# Bus Colours
# RECO...

## LONDON'S BUSES

## Kevin Lane

LONDON

IAN ALLAN LTD

Previous page:

*London United's Routemasters are scheduled only from Shepherds Bush garage, on routes 9, 10, 12, 88 and 94. RML2704 stands in traffic in the Strand on a 9, while immediately behind is a South Yorkshire Transport Atlantean, on hire to London & Country and working a 176 to Oxford Circus in December 1990. The Atlanteans returned to their owner when new Volvo Citybuses were delivered.* Kevin Lane

First published 1991

ISBN 0 7110 1997 5

© Ian Allan Ltd 1991

Published by Ian Allan Ltd, Shepperton, Surrey; and printed by Ian Allan Printing Ltd at their works at Coombelands in Runnymede, England

British Library Cataloguing in Publication Data

Lane, Kevin
  London's buses. – (Bus & coach recognition)
  I. Title II. Series
  388.32209421

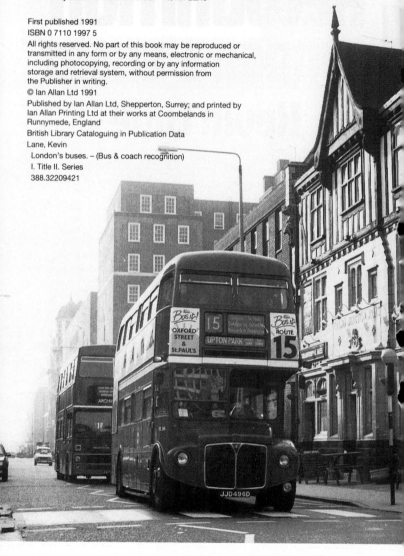

# CONTENTS

Left:
*Another Routemaster, this time on the other side of London, RML2496 of Upton Park garage heads for home past the rather attractive Grand Junction Arms, Paddington, which reflects the canal history of the area.*
Kevin Lane

# Introduction

It is probably safe to say, that 20 years ago this type of book would not have been written (quite apart from the fact that I was only 15 years old!) A glance through the pages of the 1971 Ian Allan *London Buses* pocket-book would reveal comparatively little vehicular variety: the LTE (ie red) fleet consisted of 15 classes — RM/RML/FRM/RT/RLH/DMS/ XA/RTL/RTW/RF/MB/MBA/MBS/SM/SMS — with several additional types working in the London Country fleet. In complete contrast, the 1990 Capital Transport *London Bus Handbook* lists over 50 classes in London Buses Ltd (to which more have been added subsequently), not considering those independent operators working tendered contracts on behalf of LT. Some difference! This is not to imply that 1971 was uninteresting in London — it most certainly was not — but you will see my point. Admittedly, some would not swap a single RT for any number of minibuses, but you can't win them all.

With the London bus scene at its most interesting stage, perhaps ever, this book is an endeavour to gather the kind of information useful to a bus enthusiast visiting London.

The book is divided into two main parts, the first dealing with the various operators that work services either within, or in from outside, London, and a look at coaching, sightseeing buses, etc; while the second part gives practical advice on where to go and what to see. Information on tickets and timetables is also included.

I must admit that a book of this sort would have been useful to me in 1979. My interest in buses at that time suffered through a lack of knowledge, and as a consequence I did not know where to find the last RT and RF types that were in their last weeks of service. I tracked the RFs down to ground in Kingston, but the RTs eluded me altogether. Whilst I hope that this book will appeal to those living outside London, enthusiasts within London may find something new also.

## Acknowledgements

Many people have helped with information and suggestions during the preparation of this book, including Stephen Morris and Roy Waterhouse and the numerous bus companies and others who have supplied an awful lot of useful material. Thank you. Maureen, my wife, has been on hand with tea and criticism, usually on the noise of my typewriter and general untidiness of my work room: thank you too!

*Kevin Lane*
Dunstable
September 1991

Left:
*No prizes for guessing the location of this! Grey Green Volvo Citybus 120 negotiates Parliament Square in the gathering gloom of a January afternoon on a Pimlico-bound 24.*
Kevin Lane

Front cover:
*London United's M889 is seen here at Putney Bridge on 3 November 1990 whilst on route 220.* Kevin Lane

Back cover, top:
*Selkent's DW63 seen in Ladywell Road on 28 April 1991 whilst on route P4.*
R. J. Waterhouse

Back cover, bottom:
*A large number of London Buses are now in the hands of preservationists and present interesting opportunities for the photographer. RM613 and RM14 stand outside the Royal Forest Hotel, Chingford on 12 May 1991.* Andrew Smith

Above:
*Stanwell Bus Company's Titan T971 seen in full Westlink livery at Kingston station in September 1991.* Stephen C. Morris

## References

The following publications have proved invaluable in the compilation of this book:

*London Bus Handbook* (Parts 1 & 2): Capital Transport Publishing.
*Traditional Independents: Bus & Coach Fleets, Traffic Area N — Metropolitan*: D. J. Slater.
*London Transport Route Working Index SUP 29B*: London Omnibus Traction Society.
*London Buses Fleet List SUP 17Q*: London Omnibus Traction Society.
*London Transport Bus Garages Since 1948*: Ian Allan Ltd.

The news sheets of the PSV circle have been extensively consulted, as have the various timetables and publicity brochures published by London Buses, Surrey CC, Hertfordshire CC, Essex CC, etc. Mention should also be made of the 'Londoners' Omnibus' column in *Buses* magazine.

## Transport Bookshops

The following bookshops stock a range of transport books that is more comprehensive than the average High Street outlet:

Ian Allan Bookshop, 45/46 Lower Marsh, Waterloo.
The Smokebox, Cromwell Road, Kingston (opposite Kingston bus garage).
DPR Marketing & Sales, 37 Heath Road, Twickenham.
Motor Books, 33 St Martins Court, WC2 (off Charing Cross Road).
Lens of Sutton, 4 Westmead Road, Sutton.
Foyles, Charing Cross Road, WC2.
London Transport Travel Shop, 55 Broadway Shopping Mall, St James's Park station (Monday to Friday only).

# LONDON BUS UNITS

# Centrewest London Buses Ltd

*Telstar House, Eastbourne Terrace, W2*

Heading westwards from Westbourne Park, Centrewest's territory extends to Uxbridge including Alperton, Ealing and Ruislip, thus embracing the Uxbridge area minibus scheme (U-Line), the Ealing area E routes, and also Gold Arrow midibus routes 28/31.

Most services are fairly localised, although there are a number of trunk routes including the 18 (Sudbury-Farringdon Street) and Routemaster-worked 7 (East Acton-Bloomsbury), and 15 (Ladbroke Grove-East Ham), the latter shared with East London. Five night routes are operated: perhaps the longest is the N18 (Victoria Station/Trafalgar Square-Watford Junction), worked by the standard Centrewest double-decker, the Metrobus.

The Uxbridge area U-Line network consists of routes U1-U5 and uses Uxbridge garage's allocation of Alexander-bodied Mercedes 811D midibuses, together with the lone MTL type, a MB811D with Reeve-Burgess Beaver bodywork. More MAs are at Westbourne Park for the Gold Arrow 28/31 routes, converted from Routemaster operation in March/April 1989 and now being supplanted by DW class, Wright-bodied Dennis Darts, with Irish registrations. Currently there are eight Ealing area E routes, mostly midibus-worked, which along with the 282 sees the RW class, Wright-bodied Renault 50s, again immediately recognisable by their Irish registrations.

There are garages at Acton Town, Hanwell, Alperton, Uxbridge and Westbourne Park.

*Above:*
*The Metrobus is the standard Centrewest double-decker, six of which are seen inside Alperton garage in April 1990. The centre pair, M157 and M260, have worked the 92, now in the hands of London Buslines.*   Kevin Lane

Previous page:
*A small allocation of Routemasters work off Westbourne Park garage, including RML2486 pictured in Ladbrook Grove on a 7 in January 1991.*   Kevin Lane

Above:
*A new class to enter service in London in 1990 was the DW-Wright-bodied Dennis Darts. Centrewest began using the type on the 297 (Ealing Broadway-Willesden) from 1 December. DW3 is seen passing Wembley Park station during its initial week in service.* Kevin Lane

Below:
*The Uxbridge are a U-Line network uses the MA class, Alexander-bodied Mercedes-Benz 811Ds. MA66 is pictured at West Drayton station on a U5 (Uxbridge-Stockley Park) journey in December 1990.* Kevin Lane

# East London Bus & Coach Company Ltd

*16-20 Clements Road, Ilford, Essex IG1 1BA*

As its name would imply, East London's area is just that, from the East End and extendin into Essex, including Ilford and Romford. As one of the largest of the bus operating units East London operates local routes in Docklands, Stratford, Ilford, Barking and Romfor with a number of longer routes taking buses into central and north London, for example th 25 (Victoria-Becontree Heath), Titan-worked and shared between Bow and West Ham Night routes also feature, as does a network of mobility routes in the Redbridge, Haverin and Barking areas. East London is also responsible for Docklands Light Railway replace ment services, when the line is closed for maintenance, etc, on evenings and at weekends.

As far as vehicles go, East London is very much the land of the Titan, with over 300 i stock, represented at all garages, with most at West Ham. T1-T41 are at Romford, while th last of London's RTs were ousted by the type at Barking in 1979. Unusual members of th type include open-top T512, and a former West Midlands machine, T1128 which has coac seating and sees use as a private hire vehicle.

Routemasters still work off Bow and Upton Park, on the 8 and 15/15B/X15 respectively The X15 of course has used former Green Line RMCs in their attractive gold-lined livery with RMA8, in a livery for East London Coaches, used as back-up, but Titans were due t take over here in November 1991. The X15, or Beckton Express, runs during the pea hours, Monday to Friday, and hourly (six return journeys), on Saturdays.

There are Leyland Nationals at West Ham for the D5 (Mile End-Isle of Dogs, Asda), whic are lined out in gold and look quite attractive, and also for the mobility routes. Minibuses ar confined to the 100 (Liverpool Street-Shadwell), 276 (North Woolwich-Stoke Newingtor and S2 (Stratford-Clapton), all working from Bow with RB class Renaults and SR clas Optare StarRiders.

East London has garages at Seven Kings, Barking, Bow, Romford, Upton Park and Wes Ham, and from 23 November 1991, took over Leyton from London Forest. At the same time some of Forest's services from Ash Grove (D1, D6, part of 6 and 30) were taken over, work ing from West Ham and Bow.

eft:
itans T1-T41 are all at Romford. T2 is seen leaving Newbury Park bus station on a 296
urney from Ilford to Harold Hill.   Kevin Lane

op:
ast London Leyland Nationals are to be found at only Romford and West Ham; in the
rmer case, they are mobility buses only. Most of those at West Ham have a special
old-lined livery, including LS245 nearing the Isle of Dogs Asda store.   Kevin Lane

bove:
ll of East London's midibuses are RB class Reeve-Burgess-bodied Renault 50s: this is
B19 waiting at Stratford on a Clapton-bound S2.   Kevin Lane

# Leaside Bus Co Ltd

*Manor House Office, 279 Seven Sisters Road, N4 1QC*

Leaside operates over 30 routes in the Enfield, Palmers Green, Wood Green and Tottenham areas, as well as a number of trunk routes — the 29 (Victoria-Enfield), for example. The longest route is actually night route N90 (Victoria Station-Hammond Street), a distance 22¼ miles, while the shortest, at just under six miles, is the 41 (Archway Station-Tottenham Ferry Lane). In contrast to these urban routes, Leaside also operates a summer only 'Leisure Bus' 333 from Mile End to Waltham Abbey giving access to the Lee Valley Park, a well as a full programme of tours and excursions.

The Routemaster still figures in the Leaside fleet, 35 RMLs being required for the 7 (Victoria Station-Stoke Newington) at Tottenham. Also owned is the first production Routemaster, RM5, in showbus condition, which is reserved for special duties. With the exception of open-top DMS2291, a regular on the 333, the fleet is Metrobuses and more Metrobuses! There is some variety, however: M1443-M1447 at Wood Green are ex-Greater Manchester machines, while M1437 at Stamford Hill has a turbocharged engine and coach seats. Single-deck vehicles are a couple of Leyland Nationals and Wright-bodied Denni Darts, the latter used on the 84A (Turnpike Lane-Arkley). There are also a pair of Plaxton bodied Leyland Tigers, bought new in 1989. An interesting member of the service fleet is former East Kent AEC Regent V used for driver training.

Operations are now conducted from six garages: Palmers Green, Tottenham, Enfield, Stanford Hill and Wood Green plus, from 23 November 1991, Hackney (may be renamed Clapton), latterly a London Forest garage.

Above:
*The Metrobus reigns almost supreme in the Leaside double-deck fleet and is represented a all garages. Typical is M539 leaving Walthamstow Central bus station for Barnet.* Kevin Lane

Above:
*Routemasters are confined to Tottenham for the 73. RML2373 is pictured in Islington, Victoria-bound.*   Kevin Lane

Below:
*Wright-bodied Dennis Darts now work the 84A. DW51 passes Wood Green when new, in March 1991.*   Kevin Lane

# London Central Bus Co Ltd

*Riverdale Office Centre, 68 Molesworth Street, Lewisham SE13 7EW*

London Central is not quite that. Based in Lewisham, South London, the bulk of its operations run from that area into the West End, although the recent acquisitions of Selkent's Bexleyheath garage, along with many of its routes, has pushed it eastwards. Longer-haul routes include the 12 (East Acton-Dulwich), 141 (Wood Green-Grove Park) and the various night routes, not least the NX1, Trafalgar Square-Gillingham! Several midibus routes are operated, mostly P routes off Peckham garage, which also works a network of mobility routes. Contract and private hire is promoted as London Central Travel.

The majority of the double-deck fleet is composed of Titans, although New Cross has a small allocation of Olympians. Routemasters of both RM and RML variants are represented at Peckham and Camberwell, and see use on the 3/12/36/36A/36B routes: indeed, the 36 group must have the largest concentrations of the RM type in London. Midibuses are Optare StarRiders and Metroriders, while the mobility buses are, as elsewhere, converted Leyland Nationals. Available on the coaching side is a former London Country North East Leyland Tiger, while Olympian L261 and former West Midlands Titan T1129 also have coach seating.

Garages are at New Cross, Peckham, Camberwell and Bexleyheath.

Above:
*London Central has nearly 200 Leyland Titan double-deckers, two of which, T993 and T966, sit outside Camberwell garage in July 1990. The chosen logo, the Cutty Sark, is quite prominent on both buses and the building.*   Kevin Lane

Below:

*In an interesting initiative, London Central began route NX1 from Trafalgar Square to the Medway towns, rather out of its traditional operating area. Coach-seated Leyland Olympian L261, carrying the registration number from RM1002, stands in Gillingham on 20 October 1990.* R. J. Waterhouse

Bottom:

*RML2275 has non-opening front upper-deck windows, and is illustrated here on a 159 at West Hampstead in July 1990.* Kevin Lane

# London Coaches Ltd

*Jews Row, Wandsworth SW18 1TB*

Originally known as the Commercial Operations Unit, the London Coaches title appeared in October 1986, and was responsible for sightseeing and private hire work.

Today, a varied fleet of Routemasters are available for use on the Original London Sightseeing Tour (described later in the book) and London Plus, a new hop-on, hop-off tourist route started in late-August 1991, including RMs, RMs with RMC rear ends, and RCLs; and the latest variant, the ERM, a standard Routemaster rebuilt with an additional full bay which increases its total seating capacity by eight. More modern double-deckers are the three H-class Dennis Dominators, transferred from South London. There are also some convertible open-top Routemasters.

On the actual coaching side, there is a network of commuter routes between London and northwest Kent which originated with routes taken over from Bexleyheath Transport in 1988. The current services are:

P1-4 Northfleet-Gravesend-Victoria
R1-4 Northfleet-Singlewell-Victoria
S1-3 Singlewell-Victoria
V1-3 Borough Green-Meopham-Victoria

In addition to the above, a service is provided for the New Ash Green Commuter Club from New Ash Green to Victoria. Contracts include those for the Japanese school, Acton, and the Digby Stuart College, Roehampton, the latter using a pair of Volvo B10Ms acquired from the college.

The 'standard' coach is the DV class, Van Hool-bodied DAFs, although other combinations include DAF/Duple, Volvo/Duple and Tiger/Duple. Vehicles are garaged at Wandsworth, with several outstations in Kent.

London Coaches Ltd is the first part of London Buses to be put up for sale to the private sector, presaging the privatisation of the company as a whole over the next few years.

Above:
*London Coaches is responsible for vehicles on the Round London Sightseeing Tour. Here RM237 bowls along the Embankment on a fine spring day in 1989.* Kevin Lane

Left:
*DD3 is a Duple-bodied DAF SB2300, here seen at Wilton Road coach station, Victoria, prior to working an evening commuter journey to the Medway Towns.* Kevin Lane

# London Forest Travel Ltd

*The Old Tramways Office, Chingford Road, Walthamstow E17 4PN*

London Forest was one of the smaller bus units, occupying an area of northeast London stretching from Hackney to Walthamstow and beyond. A number of trunk routes were operated, including two with Routemasters, the 6 (Kensal Green-West End-Hackney Wick) shared with Metroline and the 38 (Victoria-Clapton). Another notable route was the D1 Docklands Express, Titan-worked off Ash Grove, between Waterloo and the Isle of Dogs, Harbour Exchange Square.

It became a victim of the tendering system, and a strike over new conditions at Walthamstow led to the loss of all Walthamstow's 11 routes. As a result Walthamstow and Ash Grove, a large garage in Hackney, opened as recently as 1981 to replace Hackney and Dalton, closed from 23 November 1991, and its two other garages were added to neighbouring London Buses units. Thus Leyton (which had been expected to close, but has a stay of execution for the time being) has gone to East London and Hackney, which is actually a reopened Clapton and not to be confused with the original Hackney garage, has gone to Leaside. The Ash Grove services have been redistributed amongst East London, Leaside and London Central, with the 106 going to Hackney, now in Leaside. Thus London Forest ceased to exist from 23 November 1991 after a rather sorry recent past.

Above:
*Leyland Titans accounted for all London Forest rear-engined double-deckers, now operated by East London from West Ham. T827 is one of those dedicated for use on the D1 Docklands Express, and is seen at Waterloo in December 1990.* Kevin Lane

Above:
*Photographed when brand new in February 1990, TPL3 is a Plaxton-bodied Leyland Tiger.*
R. J. Waterhouse

Below:
*Routemasters were provided for the 6 and 38. This is RM1676 heading a bus-jam (caused by a failed Titan) in New Oxford Street in the summer of 1990* Kevin Lane

# London General Transport Services Ltd

*London General House, 25 Raleigh Gardens, Mitcham, Surrey CR4 3NS*

London General's area is quite diverse, stretching from Victoria, in central London, down through the southwestern suburbs to Sutton and beyond into Surrey. Local identities used are Suttonbus, Red Arrow and Streetline. Several routes are supported by Surrey County Council, including the 522 (evenings and Sundays) from Sutton all the way to Gatwick Airport. Rather more urban is the Red Arrow network, all routes except one (503) running between main railway stations. Minibuses, operating from the basement at Victoria, work the 239 (MA class), 153 and C1/2/3 (SR and MRL classes) as well as the Carelink service, a wheelchair facility linking Waterloo, Victoria, Paddington, Euston, King's Cross and Liverpool Street stations. Three OVs and a CVE Omni have been converted for this use. At Sutton there are three Metroriders, whose use includes the 352 and Surrey CC routes, while the 39 requires eight MAs at Putney.

London General's fleet of Routemasters is a familiar sight throughout central London, working routes 11/14/19/22/88, with a roughly equal mix of RMs and RMLs. However, London General has the most DMSs of any unit, over 200, allocated to Sutton, Merton and Stockwell garages. Metrobuses are operated also, as well as over 60 Volvo Citybuses, bought for tendered routes 133 and 196, worked off Stockwell. Apart from the minibuses mentioned above, the only single-deckers at present are the fleet of Leyland National 2s used on Red Arrow services.

Buses are garaged at Sutton, Colliers Wood, Putney, Merton, Victoria, Victoria Basement, Stockwell and Waterloo (Red Arrow).

Left:
*London General RM1015 comes off Battersea Bridge with a short working on route 19 from Clapham Junction. This vehicle is very rare in that it is one of only a handful of Leyland-engined Routemasters to survive withdrawal.* Kevin Lane

Top:
*The VC class of Northern Counties-bodied Volvo Citybuses are regular performers on routes 133 and 196. VC2, which along with a couple of others has coach seating on the upper deck and bus seating on the lower, was having a day out at the seaside at Brighton in September 1990.* Kevin Lane

Above:
*Reeve-Burgess-bodied Dennis Darts are becoming common in certain parts of London, including Clapham Junction, where London General DR43 is seen working a Wimbledon-bound 156, previously a double-deck turn.* Kevin Lane

Above:
*London General still has over 200 DMS class Daimler Fleetlines in service, operating from Sutton, Merton and Stockwell. DMS2367, with SuttonBus local identity, is seen at Morden in November 1990.   Kevin Lane*

Below:
*London General works the Red Arrow services, using Leyland National 2s. LS491, notable in having a dot-matrix destination display, is seen sitting in the sun at Marble Arch during the summer of 1989.   Kevin Lane*

# London Northern Bus Co Ltd

*Hobson House, 155 Gower Street, WC1E 6LD*

London Northern's operating area is long and thin, stretching approximately from central London to Potters Bar and beyond into Hertfordshire, including St Albans, Hertford and Harlow, via the likes of Barnet, Finchley and Hampstead, resulting in a fair mixture of urban and rural operations.

The fleet of around 300 vehicles, although dominated by the Titan and Metrobus, has some variety within its ranks. Holloway garage has a handful of second-hand Metrobuses, originating with West Yorkshire PTE and acquired from its successor, Yorkshire Rider, and from Busways. The numbers of Volvos in the fleet has declined to just V1-3, bought new in 1984, with the withdrawal of former South Yorkshire and West Midlands PTE examples late in 1990. However, Potters Bar also has nine Scania N112s for service on tendered route 263 (Archway-Barnet/Potters Bar). Rounding off the double-deckers come the Route-masters, almost all of them RMLs, which work off Finchley on the 13 (North Finchley-Aldwych) and Holloway on the 10 (Hammersmith-Tufnell Park).

By late 1990 the single-deck requirements of London Northern became minimal with the loss of the C11 and 210 tender earlier in the year. Nevertheless, there are several midibus routes in operation, requiring Metroriders and StarRiders from Potters Bar. An interesting coach now in the fleet is SKY 1, a Neoplan Skyliner.

London Northern has garages at Chalk Farm, Holloway, Finchley and Potters Bar.

Above:
*RML903 has been a showbus and still retains gold fleetnames, but is looking a bit the worse for wear in this view at Piccadilly Circus in October 1990 while working a 13 from North Finchley.* Kevin Lane

Above:
*London Northern's midibus requirement is currently confined to the several routes from Potters Bar garage. MCW Metrorider MR26 turns into Barnet High Street to return to Cockfosters in December 1990.* Kevin Lane

Below:
*At Waterloo station, about to depart for Archway, is London Northern's Leyland Titan T311.* Kevin Lane

# London United Busways Ltd

*Busway House, Wellington Road, Twickenham TW2 5NX*

London United's operating area is to the southwest of London, including Hounslow, Twickenham, Richmond, Kingston and Heathrow, although a number of trunk routes penetrate Central London. Local identities used are Riverside Bus on the 237/283 at Stamford Brook and Harrier at Fulwell and Hounslow. Stamford Brook is also responsible for Airbus routes A1/A2 and A3, the latter a new service to Stansted, from Chiswick.

The double-deck allocation is predominantly Metrobus, although RMLs still figure in the fleet, all at Shepherds Bush, for routes 9/10/12/88/94. Twenty Olympians with Leyland bodies work on the 237.

Apart from a few LS class Leyland Nationals the single-deckers are five Lynxes at Stamford Brook for the 190. Small buses are mainly Dennis Darts, whose duties include the former Scancoaches route 283 famed for its Jonckheere-bodied Scanias. The H24/5 is using Reeve-Burgess-bodied Ivecos with wheelchair facilities.

Finally, an AEC Reliance and four Leopard coaches are at Norbiton.

Buses are garaged at Hounslow, Fulwell, Norbiton, Shepherds Bush and Stamford Brook (although Norbiton is scheduled for closure).

Above:
*London United is responsible for the Airbus routes, which work from Stamford Brook garage. The A1 and A2 have a dedicated fleet of Metrobuses, while the short-lived A3 required Leyland Olympians. L312 passes through Hammersmith with the 14.26 Stamford Brook garage to Stansted.*   Kevin Lane

Above:
*The newest London United Busways double-deckers are the 23 Olympians at Stamford Brook, bought for the 237 Riverside Bus operation in 1989. L304 stands at Sunbury Village in November 1990.* Kevin Lane

Above right:
*Leyland Lynxes entered service on the 283 in 1989, a tendered route operated formerly by Scancoaches. LX3, with Riverside Bus fleetnames, is seen at Hammersmith Butterwick in April 1990. The type is now used on the 190, too.* Kevin Lane

Right:
*Although no longer in passenger service, the BL class of Bristol LH/ECW single-deckers still see a limited role as driver trainers. London United BL33 is seen in Hounslow.* Kevin Lane

27

# Metroline Travel Ltd

*118-122 College Road, Harrow, Middlesex HA1 1DB*

Metroline operates in the Harrow, Edgware and Willesden areas of northwest London. Much of this is urban in nature, although there are plenty of attractive corners in this heart of 'Metroland'. A number of longer routes extend out of the area, such as the 6 (Kensal Green-City-Hackney Wick), RML-worked off Willesden and shared with London Forest's Ash Grove garage which has the majority of the work.

The dominant type in the fleet is the Metrobus, including the first five which are still at Cricklewood after 13 years and are easily identified by their small route boxes. The only other double-deckers at present are a small number of RMLs for the 6 at Willesden, following the withdrawal of Harrow's Mk II Metrobuses and former West Midlands Volvo Ailsas brought about by the loss of tendered work in 1990/91. The Dennis Dart has quickly established itself in the fleet, with members of the DT class operating from all garages except Cricklewood. There are also a few Leyland Nationals.

Buses operate from Willesden, Edgware, Harrow Weald, North Wembley and Cricklewood.

Below:
*Metroline has only a small allocation of Routemasters, found at Willesden for the 6, which is shared with Ash Grove (London Forest). RML2404 has left the rear of its home garage and is seen in Pound Lane in February 1991.* Kevin Lane

Top:
*The earliest Metrobuses are at Cricklewood; they are recognisable by their smaller destination display. M2 is working a 266 at Willesden Green in April 1990.* Kevin Lane

Above:
*Dennis Darts are now common on Harrow area H routes; DT138 here picking up passengers at Rayners Lane while working an H12 in February 1991.* Kevin Lane

# South East London & Kent Bus Co Ltd

*68 Molesworth Street, Lewisham, SE13 7EU*

The South East London & Kent Bus Co Ltd is more commonly known as Selkent. As it name suggests, it occupies the southeastern corner of London down to the Kent borde and beyond, to include Woolwich, Orpington, Bromley and Catford. Selkent was former strong in and around the Bexley area, but the Bexleyheath operations, including the garage were lost to London Central following retendering in January 1991. The loss of Bexleybu leaves just one local identity, that of Roundabout in Orpington.

The actual operating area is quite diverse, with busy trunk routes such as the 1 (Trafalga Square-Bromley Common) and the 53 (Oxford Circus-Plumstead Common), Titan an Olympian-worked respectively, down to the midibus routes around Bromley and Orpington. The Olympians include a trio of coach-seated examples carrying former Routemaster regis trations, and L136 which carries a special livery of red, cream and grey, celebrating the cer tenary of tram operation in Lewisham. Routemasters are confined to Catford for use on the 36B, which it shares with Peckham, Mondays to Saturdays. There is also a DMS, converte to open-top, for use by Selkent Travel. Single-deck vehicles comprise a number of Leyland Nationals and an Optare Delta at Bromley.

The Dennis Dart is a popular choice at the moment, with a number now in service. The are common in the Bromley area, while the Orpington area network includes Ivecos an Mercedes. Catford garage has Optare StarRiders for several local routes, carrying a blac cat motif, as do the Wright-bodied Mercedes there also. Selkent has a Leyland Tiger coac in its private hire fleet.

Selkent has garages at Orpington, Plumstead, Catford and Bromley.

Above:
*The only Selkent Routemasters scheduled for service are those at Catford for the 36B: RM449, devoid of any exterior advertisements, heads for Grove Park in Lewisham in the summer of 1990.   Kevin Lane*

Left:
*Plumstead has the largest allocation of Leyland Olympians, two of which, L76 and L70, are seen in New Cross on 188 and 177 workings, the former route being operated previously by Boro'line.   Kevin Lane*

Top:
*Selkent has the first DAF Optare Delta, DA1, currently at Bromley. It is used primarily on private hire duties, but was photographed on local route B1 in Westmoreland Road in December 1989.* R. J. Waterhouse

Above:
*Dennis Darts are also in favour with Selkent, with allocations at both Bromley and Orpington. DT37 is one of the latter, complete with Roundabout fleetnames, and is seen in Sidcup on an R11 to Green Street Green in October 1990.* Kevin Lane

# South London Transport Ltd

*Sycamore House, London Road, Thornton Heath CR4 6AW*

The operating area of South London stretches from central London, down through Brixton and Streatham to Croydon and beyond. Although the company takes Tower Bridge as its logo, none of its routes pass over it.

The network contains a number of trunk roads, taking buses out of their area — for example, the 159 (West Hampstead-Streatham), which is still Routemaster-worked and shared with London Central's Camberwell garage. Other Routemaster duties are the 2B (Crystal Palace-Baker Street) and 137 (Crystal Palace-Oxford Circus).

The double-deck fleet also contains Leyland Olympians — including six at Norwood (166-71) with coach seating for peak-hour service X68 — Metrobuses and DMSs.

There is an allocation of Leyland Nationals at Croydon, while Streatham has Metroriders for the 115/366/367/G1/G2, the latter operated in conjunction with Wandsworth Area Health Authority. Dennis Darts are scheduled on tendered route 412 and the 64 on Sundays.

There are five South London garages: Streatham, Norwood, Croydon, Brixton and Thornton Heath.

Below:
*Routemasters, of both RM and RML varieties, still feature well in the South London fleet, operating from Streatham, Brixton and Norwood garages. RM173 paces a cyclist along West End Lane, West Hampstead on a 159 in March 1989.*   Kevin Lane

Above:
*The most numerous type in the South London fleet is the Leyland Olympian, with over 100 r service. L178 and L2 are seen at Euston station on the long 68 route to Croydon, the latter vehicle being one of three delivered in 1984 as an evaluatory vehicle in the Alternative Vehicle Programme, alongside the Mk 2 Metrobus, Dennis Dominator and Volvo Ailsa.* Kevin Lane

Below:
*The Tower Bridge logo is quite prominent on the front of Dennis Dart DT62 of Thornton Heath, working tendered route 412 at Purley.* Colin Stannard

# Stanwell Bus Company

*6 Pulborough Lane, Green Lane, Hounslow TW4 6DE*

Stanwell Buses, trading as Westlink, pre-dates the present bus operating units. This subsidiary of London Buses was set up in 1986 in order to work services won by tender from Surrey County Council, initially the 116/117/203 using Leyland Nationals. Operations have subsequently expanded to include additional Surrey County Council routes together with some LRT tendered services also. This has resulted in red buses appearing in some pretty far-flung places, with infrequent services to match. Downside and Cobham, for example, are reached for times a day from Kingston on the 513, while the 500 manages to get from Staines to Bagshot but twice a day.

More frequent are the various Kingston area K routes, using Metroriders. Other routes of interest are the 110, with its DAF Optare Deltas, Dennis Darts on the 371, and the distinctive CVE Omni on the H20, operated by Westlink although the vehicles are owned by the London Borough of Hounslow.

For further variety, look out for FS29 on former Fountain Luxury Coaches route 602 (this service and others are included in the Surrey County Council Elmbridge, Runnymede and Spelthorne timetable book). From September 1990, Westlink took over LRT tendered route 131 from London & Country, shipping in Leyland Titans, previously unknown in these parts, thus commencing double-deck operation for the first time, although the 116/7 and 203 passed to other operators from 10 August 1991. Also of interest are the Austin FX4 taxis, some in full fleet livery, used for staff transfer, etc, from the garage near Hounslow Heath. The other garage is at Kingston.

Above:
*The 110 was another route won by Westlink from London & Country by tender, this time in April 1990. DAF Optare Deltas were bought for this service: DA2 was caught by the camera on a bleak December morning loading for Twickenham at Hounslow bus station.*
Kevin Lane

Above:
*Westlink operates the long version of the Wright-bodied Dennis Dart, illustrated here by DWL11 in Richmond.   Colin Stannard*

Below:
*The three CVE Omni minibuses operated by Westlink are in fact owned by the London Borough of Hounslow, and are used on local service H20. Two of the three are in white livery, shown here by CV1 in Lampton Road in December 1990. With the future of the CVE Omni in doubt, the four in London service (one is also used on Carelink duties) may remain unique.   Kevin Lane*

# LT
# CONTRACT
# OPERATORS

# Armchair Passenger Transport

*Brent Way, Brentford, Middx TW8 8ES*

The orange and white coaches of Armchair have been a familiar sight around London on private hire and contract duties for some years. Interest increased for the enthusiast during the late 1980s with the operation of former Green Line routes 733 (Hitchin-Watford) and 750/1 (Heathrow-Ware), although both have subsequently been lost. Local bus operation began in August 1987 with Surrey County Council contracts for the 555/556/557, currently using Wadham Stringer-bodied Leyland Swifts.

More prominence came with the awarding of LT contracts for the 260 and 65 in 1990, although the latter was worked by London & Country for the initial six months. Twelve new Leyland Olympians were bought for the 260, with a trio of re-registered former South Yorkshire Atlanteans as back-up.

### LT Tendered Routes

65 Ealing Broadway-Kingston (daily) from 25.1.91 (originally operated by London Buses/Kingston Bus from 27.6.87, temporary contract by London & Country from 29.9.90)

260 Shepherds Bush-North Finchley (daily) from 23.6.90

Above:
*Armchair's first LT contract was for the 260, for which Leyland Olympians were bought in 1990. Alexander-bodied G366 YUR is pictured in a damp Shepherds Bush in September 1990, complete with an incorrect blind spelling.* Kevin Lane

Previous page:
*Leyland Olympians were bought for the 65: H552 GKX is seen in the pouring rain at South Ealing on 1 February 1991, during its first week in service.* Kevin Lane

# Atlas Bus

*80 Old Oak Common Lane, London W3 7DA*

Panatlas Leisure Ltd, previously a coach operator, won the contract to operate the 112 from July 1988, using eight Leyland Lynxes, to be followed by the 107 in October 1989, this time employing Leyland Olympians with bodies by Northern Counties. Also in stock is an Olympian demonstrator, an ex-West Midlands Leyland Fleetline and a Leyland National, new to Cumberland. The coaching fleet is currently Leyland Tiger and several varieties of DAF.

Vehicles operate from Atlas Road, NW10 and Waterloo Road, Uxbridge.

**LT Tendered Routes**
107 New Barnet-Queensbury (daily) from 7.10.89 (formerly London Buses from 27.9.86)
112 Ealing Broadway-Wood Green (Mon-Sat) from 30.7.88

Below:
*Nine Leyland Olympians with Northern Counties bodywork were bought by Atlas Bus for use on the 107. AB68 is in Borehamwood on its way to New Barnet on a bleak December day in 1990.* Kevin Lane

Above:
*This former Leyland Olympian demonstrator is also in Atlas Bus stock and is seen at the Queensbury terminus of the 107 in the company of one of the Northern Counties-bodied examples.*   Kevin Lane

Below:
*The first tendered route to be operated by Atlas Bus was the 112, with Leyland Lynx single deckers bought for the purpose. AB53 arrives at Wood Green in March 1991.*   Kevin Lane

# Boro'line Maidstone

*Armstrong Road, Maidstone, Kent ME15 6TY*

On the face of it, perhaps the least likely of the current operators, Boro'line Maidstone won its first tenders in 1988 with the 132/228/328 and 233 in the January, to be followed by the 188/422 and 492 in the November. This gave the company a firm foothold in southeast London, requiring additional depots in Crayford and Greenwich, although the 188 made it all the way to Euston, causing extra excitement by initially using hired Leyland Atlanteans from Ipswich. The 108, gained a year later, did rather better by managing to get all the way from Lewisham to Wanstead via the Blackwall Tunnel, thus allowing the spectacle of a Kentish operator with municipal ancestry on local service in East London — try predicting that 10 years ago!

A varied fleet is provided for tendered services. Leyland Lynxes can be found on the 108, with former London LS class Leyland Nationals on the 492. Double-deck requirements are catered for by unusual Optare-bodied Olympians, Volvo Citybuses, a pair of Scanias and ex-Tayside Volvo Ailsas, all with Alexander bodywork, together with the Atlanteans hired from Ipswich. However, with the loss of the 188 in November 1990, there will be no doubt a cascading of vehicles, resulting in the withdrawal of the older types.

Above:
*With the loss of the contract to work the 188, the Alexander-bodied Volvo Citybuses bought for the service have moved on to other routes. Still bearing vinyls for the 188, although somewhat submerged by grime, 924 works a 422 in Woolwich in February 1991.*
Kevin Lane

# LT CONTRACT OPERATORS

### LT Tendered Routes
108  Lewisham-Wanstead (daily) from 25.11.89
132  Eltham Station-Bexleyheath (daily) from 16.1.88
228/ Eltham-Chislehurst-Eltham (Mon-Sat) from 16.1.88 (formerly London Buses from
328  13.7.85)
233  Eltham Station-Swanley (Mon-Sat) from 16.1.88
272  Woolwich-Thamesmead-Woolwich (daily) from 24.11.90 (formerly London Buses/
      Bexleybus from 16.1.88)
422  Woolwich-Bexleyheath (daily) from 26.11.88 (formerly London Buses/Bexleybus from
      16.1.88)
492  Sidcup-Dartford (Mon-Sat) from 26.11.88 (formerly London Buses/Bexleybus from
      16.1.88)

### Fomer Route
188  Greenwich-Euston from 19.11.88 until 24.11.90 (to London Buses/Selkent)


Below:
*The 108 is the preserve of the batch of Leyland Lynxes. Here 801 paces a Morris 1000
through Lewisham in August 1990.*   Kevin Lane

# BTS Coaches Ltd

*Station Road, Borehamwood, Hertfordshire WD6 1DF*

BTS Coaches entered LT contract services in a less than usual way, by taking over the 292 on an emergency basis following strike action by London Country North East in 1988 and subsequently carrying on with the route permanently. Scania double-deckers, bought in 1989, tend to be used on this route, while Leyland Olympians can be found on the company's second contract for LT, the 114, which commenced as part of the Harrow area changes in 1990/91.

Other contracts are currently operated on behalf of Hertfordshire County Council, including the 355 (St Albans-Borehamwood), on which the former Kelvin Scottish Metrobuses seem popular; and local minibus services in Borehamwood employing MCW Metroriders formerly operated by LCNE. The depot is adjacent to Elstree & Borehamwood station.

**LT Tendered Routes**
114 Mill Hill Broadway-Ruislip (daily) from 19.1.91
292 Borehamwood-Edgware Station (daily) from 22.2.88

Above:
*The newest buses in the BTS fleet are the batch of Northern Counties-bodied Leyland Olympians delivered early in 1991 for use on the tendered 114. H151 GGS pulls out of Harrow bus station when almost new in February 1991.* Kevin Lane

# County Bus & Coach Co Ltd

*Fourth Avenue, Harlow, Essex CM20 1DU*

County Bus & Coach has a small commitment to LT-tendered work, with just three routes currently under its operation. The company is a fairly new one, taking over the eastern part of London Country North East (the western part passing to Sovereign Bus & Coach) in 1989, with, initially, garages at Harlow, Hertford and Grays. Part of the Grays operation was split in 1990; passing initially to a company called Simco 314 including one tendered route, the 103; and passing subsequently along with the vehicles, to Grey Green.

Vehicles for the remaining tendered routes are Leyland Lynxes for the 66, and Mercedes midibuses on the 256/346.

### LT Tendered Routes
 66 Romford-Leytonstone (daily) from 4.8.90
256 Harold Hill-Hornchurch (daily) from 22.9.90 (formerly London Buses from 24.9.88)
346 Upminster Park Estate-Corbets Tey (Mon-Sat) from 22.9.90 (formerly London Buses from 24.9.88)

### Former Route
103 Rainham-North Romford (daily) from 1.9.90. To Grey Green from 6.1.91

Several new contracts have been awarded to County: W15/W16/144 (11.91) and W14 (3.92).

Above:
*Leyland Lynx LX255 is viewed across George Green, Wanstead, on a Leytonstone-bound 66 in October 1990.* Kevin Lane

# Ensign Citybus

*Arterial Road, Purfleet, Essex RM16 1TB*

Ensign must be known to most enthusiasts, not least because of its dealing activities from its Purfleet premises. Tendered services began in 1986, now covering a number of routes in the eastern part of London, including the former operations of Frontrunner South East, acquired from the Stagecoach group in 1989. Although the bus operations were acquired by the CNT Group, owners of Hong Kong Citybus, during 1990/91, neither the bus sales, together with the engineering part of Ensign, nor the London Pride Sightseeing operations, were part of the deal.

The current bus fleet is large and varied. Dennis Dominators are the latest type to arrive, and they may well spell the end of the former DMS-type Daimler Fleetlines. Both Leyland Olympians and Metrobuses have been bought new, while the secondhand market has yielded many types, including the aforementioned DMSs, further Metrobuses, plus Daimler Fleetlines, Leyland Atlanteans and a couple of Bristol VRs. Single-deckers are conspicuous by their absence. The London Pride vehicles include decapitated MCW Metroliners and DMSs. Two former London RTs are also to be noted.

Operations are conducted from a base in Dagenham, Essex.

Below:
*The newest Ensign buses are Northern Counties-bodied Dennis Dominators, including 259 carrying the new fleetname.* G. R. Mills

Above:
*Representing the DMS in the Ensign fleet is 223, working a 145 through Ilford.*   Kevin Lane

### LT Tendered Routes
   62  Barking-Gants Hill Station (daily) from 17.1.87 (since awarded to East London)
 62A  Barking-Little Heath (Mon-Sat) from 17.1.87
 165  Havering Park-Rainham (daily) from 24.9.88
 246  Harold Hill-Corbets Tey (Mon-Fri, peak hours) from 24.9.88
 248  Cranham-Romford (daily) from 1.7.89 (formerly Frontrunner from 24.9.88)
 252  Collier Row-Gidea Park (daily) from 1.7.89 (formerly Frontrunner from 3.9.88)
 347  Romford-Brentwood (Mon-Sat) from 30.10.89
 365  Havering Park-Mardyke Estate (daily) from 24.9.88
 446  Cranham-Corbets Tey (Mon-Fri, peak hours) from 24.9.88
 550  Gidea Park-Cranham (schooldays) from 3.7.89 (formerly Frontrunner from 5.9.88)
 N99  Chadwell Heath-Cranham (Fri night/Sat morning, Sat night/Sun morning) from 27.3.8

### Former Route
145  Dagenham-Redbridge (Mon-Sat) from 5.4.86. To London Buses from 22.6.91
In addition to the above, a number of contracts have been gained following their loss b
London Forest and are due to start during 11.91; 97/97A/123/158/212/215.
Wood Green area routes 153/298/299/W6 will be gained during 3.92.
Furthermore, the 62 is due to pass to East London Buses during 1.92.

# Grey Green

*53 Stamford Hill, London N16 5TD*

Grey Green has long been a familiar name in coaching. Successful LRT tenders began in February 1987 with the 173 (Stratford-Becontree Heath), dubbed, not inappropriately, 'East-enderbus'. The 125/179 followed later in the year, together with the 298/313 early in 1988.

All of the above were essentially local routes in north and east London, but in November 1988 Grey Green took charge of the 24 (Pimlico-Hampstead Heath), which brought tendering into the heart of London, and with it, an eye-catching fleet of grey, green and orange Volvo Citybuses, certainly a welcome change from the more usual sea of red!

Two routes were added in September 1990, another route through central London, the 68, again using Volvo Citybuses, and the 210, using single-deck Volvo B10Ms with distinctive East Lancs bodywork. 1991 saw the transfer of the 103 to Grey Green following a reorganisation at County Bus. Other vehicles to be found on LRT work are six Scania/East Lancs double-deckers, Fleetlines from Manchester and South Yorkshire, MCW Metrobuses also from South Yorkshire), Leyland Olympians from County Bus, and a small batch of Leyland Lynxes, the latter common on the 179 and 313.

Grey Green is also active in the commuter business, as described later, with a fleet of coaches, mainly Volvo and including a couple of double-deckers. LRT operations are carried out from a depot in Stamford Hill N16, and the former Dix site at Dagenham, while the Medway commuter services are run from one newly opened (1988) in Strood.

Below:

*Six East Lancs-bodied Scanias were bought by Grey Green in 1988. This is 112 loading in the rain at Potters Bar station, having arrived from Chingford. A London Northern Metrobus pulls in behind on a 242.*   Kevin Lane

# LT CONTRACT OPERATORS

### LT Tendered Routes

  24  Pimlico-Hampstead Heath (daily) from 5.11.88
103  Rainham-North Romford (daily) from 6.1.91 (formerly County Bus from 1.9.90)
125  North Finchley-Winchmore Hill/Enfield (daily) from 14.11.87 (formerly London Buses from 12.4.86)
168  Waterloo-Hampstead Heath (Mon-Sat) from 22.9.90
173  Stratford-Becontree Heath (Mon-Sat) from 28.2.87
179  Barking-Chingford (Mon-Sat) from 17.10.87 (formerly London Buses from 24.5.86)
210  Finsbury Park-Brent Cross (Mon-Sat) from 22.9.90
298  Turnpike Lane-South Mimms, Clare Hall Hospital (daily) from 22.2.88 (formerly London Country North East from 21.6.86)
313  Chingford-Potters Bar (Mon-Sat) from 22.2.88 (formerly London Country North East from 13.7.85)

The Wood Green area scheme, due to commence during 2.92 will see the loss of the 298 (to Ensign Citybus) and the gaining of the 141. Former Thamesway routes 20/167/235/275 will begin during 3.92.

Below:
*Further 1988 deliveries to Grey Green were Alexander-bodied Volvo Citybuses, for route 24, with further examples following in 1990 for the 168. Vehicle 118 of the earlier batch is seen at Camden Lock during the first week of the 168.*  Kevin Lane

# Kentish Bus & Coach

*Apex House, London Road, Northfleet, Kent DA11 9PD*

Kentish Bus & Coach, formerly London Country South East until 27 April 1987, has become a prominent operator of LT contracts, particularly with the awarding of central London routes 22A, 22B and 55 early in 1990. Kentish Bus is also active in the Bexley and Orpington areas and is the only non-London bus unit operator to be involved in Mobility Bus routes (although its use of red Leyland Nationals leased from LT makes this less than obvious).

A number of types can be found on London contracts: Leyland Olympians are on the 22A, 22B, 51, 51A, 55, 96 and 269, Scanias with Alexander bodies can also put in an appearance, while Optare/MCW Metroriders and Leyland Nationals can also be found. Other types, such as Leyland Atlanteans and Leyland Tigers, work on other services from outside the capital. LT operations are conducted from Leyton and Bricklayers Arms.

Below:
*Kentish Bus vehicles are now a familiar sight in central London, following the award of tenders for routes 22A/22B/55 early in 1990. Leyland Olympians are normal for these services, with 528 seen heading along Haymarket in October 1990.*   Kevin Lane

Above:
*Optare Metrorider 889 negotiates road works in Bexleyheath on a B11 in March 1991.*
Kevin Lane

### LT Tendered Routes

 20  Bromley North-Biggin Hill (Sundays) from 26.11.89 (ex-route 320)
22A Clapton Park-London Bridge station (daily) from 20.1.90
22B Homerton-Piccadilly Circus (daily) from 24.2.90
 42  Aldgate-Camberwell Green (daily) from 7.2.87
 51  Woolwich-Orpington station (daily) from 16.8.86
51A Woolwich-Swanley (Sundays) from 16.8.86
 55  Clapton-Tottenham Court Road station (daily) from 24.2.90
 96  Woolwich-Dartford (daily) from 19.1.91 (formerly London Buses/Bexleybus from 16.1.88)
269 Bexleyheath Garage-Bromley North (daily) from 19.1.91 (formerly London Buses/Bexleybus from 16.1.88)
471 Orpington station-Green Street Green (Mon-Fri peak hours) from 21.8.89 (formerly London Buses from 18.7.88)
477 Bromley North-Knockholt (Sundays) from 26.11.89
493 Orpington station-Ramsden Estate (daily) from 16.8.86
911-919 Croydon Mobility Bus routes from 26.3.90
B11 Bexleyheath-Lodge Hill (Mon-Sat) from 19.1.91 (formerly London Buses/Bexleybus from 16.1.88)
P14 Surrey Quays-Cubitt Town (daily) from 19.11.88

### Former LT Tendered Route

P4  Brixton-Lewisham from 3.8.85. To London Buses.

# London Buslines

*Middlesex Business Centre, Bridge Road, Southall, Middx UB2 4AB*

Len Wright Travel, trading as London Buslines, brought yellow ex-London DMS type Daimler Fleetlines into service in the very first round of LT tenders, in July 1985, with the winning of the 81. Further contracts have followed, with a subsequent increase in the fleet. More Daimler Fleetlines have come from Manchester, while new Leyland Lynxes have taken over on the 81. The Leyland Olympian is becoming the standard double-decker, with two batches now in service. Twenty-five-seat Mercedes-Benz are used on the C4, while over in the Richmond area, Ford Transits can be found working for the local Health Authority on routes RH1/RH2. More Mercedes were orderd for the 201 and 203 but did not arrive in time, so Dodge 50s were hired-in from South Yorkshire. Other tendered work is undertaken outside London, such as Sunday operation on local Watford routes W4/W5 on behalf of Hertfordshire County Council.

Operations are conducted from Bridge Road, Southall.

### LT Tendered Routes
79 Edgware-Alperton (Mon-Sat) from 21.11.87 (formerly London Buses 79A from 12.4.86)
81 Hounslow-Slough (daily) from 13.7.85
90 Kew Gardens Station-Yeading/Northolt (daily) from 19.8.89
92 Southall-Wembley Arena/Neasden (daily) from 10.11.90
C4 Chelsea Harbour-Putney Pier (Mon-Sat) from 1.4.89
201 Staines-Hounslow (Mon-Sat) from 10.8.91
203 Staines-Brentford (Mon-Sat) from 10.8.91

### Former LT Route
195 Charville Lane Estate-Ealing Hospital (daily) from 12.4.86. To London Buses from 13.4.91

Above:
*The 81 Hounslow-Slough was the first tender to be operated by London Buslines. Leyland Lynxes are the regular vehicles on the service today, although DMSs still appear at times. Lynx D752 DLO takes on a good load at Hounslow West.* Kevin Lane

# London & Country Greenway

*Tinsley Lane North, Crawley, West Sussex*

London & Country Greenway, the name for the eastern operating area of London Country Bus (South West), has several LT-tendered services under its belt, running from Croydon, Beddington Farm Road (127/176/289), Newington Butts (78) and Kentish Bus's Dunton Green Garage (320).

The use of brand-new buses on routes in central London has resulted in a high profile, especially taking the eye-catching two-tone green and red livery into consideration. Volvo Citybuses with East Lancs and Northern Counties bodywork tend to be used on all services except the 289, where Leyland Lynxes are to be found. However, other types can be pressed into service, including Leyland Atlanteans, which can also be seen on other, non-tendered routes, running into the London area.

### LT Tendered Routes
  78  Shoreditch-Forest Hill (daily) from 10.11.90
  85  Putney Bridge station-Kingston (daily) from 29.9.90 (formerly London Buses/Kingston Bus from 27.6.87)
 127  Selsdon/Purley-Tooting Broadway/Streatham Hill (daily) from 22.3.86
 176  Penge-Oxford Circus (daily) from 10.11.90
 289  Elmers End Green-Purley (Mon-Sat) from 7.2.87
 320  Bromley North-Biggin Hill/Westerham (Mon-Sat; Kentish Bus on Sundays) from 1.9.90

The following LT contracts have been worked previously: 110/131/196/389/393, while the 293 (Epsom-Morden) is now a commercial operation. The 65 was worked in 1990/91 on a temporary basis.

Above:
*A variety of double-deck type are used on London & Country's LT contract duties, including Volvo Citybuses with both Northern Counties and East Lancs bodywork. No 620 is one of the latter, seen at Putney Bridge station with several London Buses types, on a Kingston-bound 85 in November 1990.* Kevin Lane

# London Country North West

*Castle Street, Luton, Bedfordshire LU1 3AJ*

London Country North West, now part of the growing Luton & District empire, currently has three LT contracts, although several routes, including the minibus-operated C2, have been lost. Leyland Olympians are the standard fare on the 142 and 340, while Dennis Darts of the 9.8m variety are used on the 258.

**LT Tendered Routes**
142  Watford Junction-Edgware (daily), (Brent Cross Mon-Sat) from 22.6.86
258  Watford Junction-South Harrow (Mon-Sat) from 19.1.91
340  Edgware Station-Harrow (daily) from 19.1.91

Above:
*Leyland Olympian LR102 loads at Brent Cross on a 142 to Watford Junction. Although still in LCNW livery, the fleetnames are missing, perhaps reflecting Luton & District ownership.*
Kevin Lane

Below:
*A new class of vehicle for LCNW is of Carlyle-bodied Dennis Darts for the 258. Here DC7 loads at Harrow bus station on a South Harrow-bound journey.   Kevin Lane*

# Metrobus Ltd

*Farnborough Hill, Orpington, Kent BR6 6DA*

Metrobus is a fairly recent operator, formed by Tillingbourne (Metropolitan) Ltd (a subsidia of Tillingbourne itself), in order to take over Tillingbourne interests in the Orpington are which it did from September 1983.

Metrobus gained LRT routes 61 and 361 in August 1986, its own 353/4/7 becoming pa of the LRT network at the same time. A further LRT contract, for the 261, was gained November 1987. A number of other, non-tendered, routes are also operated.

Daimler Fleetlines from London and West Riding were amongst types in use in the ear days, but they are gradually being superseded by new and secondhand Leyland Olympian while single-deck requirements are catered for by a trio of Wadham Stringer-bodied Bec ford YMTs several Leyland Lynxes and a batch of Reeve-Burgess-bodied Dennis Dart Three coaches, all with Duple bodies, consisting of two AEC Reliances and a DAF, are als in stock, the former coming from Tillingbourne.

Metrobus was also active in Gravesend, minibus services commencing in August 198 but these passed to Kentish Bus in January 1990.

Vehicles are garaged at the former Tillingbourne premises at Farnborough Hill, Green Stre Green, near Orpington.

### LT Tendered Routes

 61  Bromley North-Chislehurst/Eltham (daily) from 16.8.86
146  Bromley North-Downe (Mon-Sat) from 10.8.91 (formerly Crystal Cars from 10.8.85)
261  Green Street Green-Lewisham (daily) from 21.11.87 (formerly London Buses fro 16.6.86)
353  Orpington-Croydon (daily) from 16.8.86
354  Bromley North-Croydon (Mon-Sat) from 16.8.86
357  Orpington-Croydon (Mon-Sat) from 16.8.86
361  Bromley North-Green Street Green (Mon-Fri) from 16.8.86

Below:
*Of the four Leyland Lynxes in the Metrobus fleet, three are second-hand, arriving from Merthyr Tydfil in 1989. D103 NDW is one such vehicle waiting at East Croydon on a 356 journey, which despite the slip-board is not an LT-tendered service.* Kevin Lane

# R&I Tours Ltd

*118 Cromwell Road, London SW7 4ET*

R&I Tours was probably little known in enthusiast circles when it was announced that it had won its first LT tenders in June 1989. However, a large mini- and midi-coach fleet was being built up, based on a variety of chassis, such as Bedford, Iveco, Toyota and Mercedes, for various duties, such as school, home-office and other contracts as well as private hire, etc.

Designated for use on the 268 are the eight 23-seat Ivecos, while the H2 sees the smaller 19-seat Ivecos. Later in 1989 came the H17, since lost to Sovereign Bus & Coach, on which Bedford/Lex single-deckers, all new to South Wales Transport, were regular performers. However, the most impressive vehicles to date are the 14 Dennis Darts, 216-229, bought in 1990 for the C11/C12 routes. All are named after castles, including 229 (*Tower of London*), while 219/220 were part of an order diverted from a Hong Kong customer. They are identified by the tinted windows and the termite-proof floors! Fleet livery is grey, blue and red and operate from Victoria Road, Park Royal.

**LT Tendered Routes**

268 Golders Green-Finchley Road station (daily) from 3.6.89 (formerly London Country North West from 31.5.86)

H2 Golders Green-Hampstead Garden Suburb-Golders Green (Mon-Sat) from 10.6.89 (formerly London Buses from 13.7.85)

C11 Archway-Brent Cross (daily, Archway-West Hampstead on Sundays) from 21.7.90

C12 King's Cross-Finchley Road station (Mon-Sat) from 21.7.90

**Former Route**

H17 Harrow-Sudbury from 2.9.89 until 16.2.91

Above:
*No 229 is one of the Dennis Darts to work the C11/C12, which R&I has operated since July 1990, displacing London Northern's Bristol LHs. It is seen in West Hampstead soon after entering service.* Kevin Lane

# Sovereign (Harrow) Ltd

*Babbage Road, Stevenage, Hertfordshire SG1 2EQ*

Sovereign (Harrow) Ltd is a subsidiary of Sovereign Bus & Coach Co Ltd, set up to operate services won by tender in the Harrow area from December 1990. An operating base has been established at the yard of Venture Transport, Pinner Road, Harrow. The initial stock consists of Reeve-Burgess-bodied Mercedes midibuses.

## LT Tendered Routes

H10  Harrow Circular (daily) from 19.1.91 (formerly Metroline/Harrow Buses from 14.11.87 as route 201)

H11  Northwick Park Hospital-Northwood station (Mon-Sat) from 1.12.90 (formerly Metroline/Harrow Buses from 14.11.87)

H13  Ruislip Lido-Northwood Hills (Mon-Sat) from 1.12.90 (formerly Metroline/Harrow Buses from 14.11.87)

H17  Harrow-Sudbury (Mon-Sat) from 16.2.91 (formerly R&I Coaches from 2.9.89)

Above:
*The H13 during the first week of Sovereign operation: a 1989 Mercedes 709D/Reeve Burgess from the parent fleet is pictured in Pembroke Road, Ruislip on 7 December 1990.*
Kevin Lane

# Tellings-Golden Miller

*20a Wintersells Road, Byfleet, Weybridge, Surrey KT14 7LF*

Tellings-Golden Miller, now part of the Midland Fox group, entered LT contract work with former Westlink routes 116/117 in the Staines area. In earlier years, when trading as simply Golden Miller, a number of local routes were operated in this part of Surrey, although just one remains, the 606 Staines to Stanwell Moor, first run in 1971. These two new contract services have been initiated using Leyland Nationals.

**LT Tendered Routes**
116  Brentford-Bedfont (daily) from 10.8.91 (formerly Westlink from 9.8.86)
117  Brentford-Staines (daily) from 10.8.91 (formerly Westlink from 9.8.86)

Below:
*Routes 116/117 employ Leyland Nationals from parent company MIdland Fox, in a blue and white livery and bearing their former fleetnumbers. 3713 is seen in Isleworth.*   Kevin Lane

# LT CONTRACT OPERATORS

## Thamesway

*48/49 New Writtle Street, Chelmsford, Essex CM2 0SD*

Thamesway was formed in July 1990 on the division of the former NBC subsidiary Eastern National, privatised in 1986 but sold to the Badgerline group in April 1990. The operation of tendered routes in London, previously marketed as Eastern National Citybus, came under Thamesway, comprising some 11 routes from bases in Walthamstow and Ponders End.

The fleet is composed of Mercedes-Benz midibuses of various types, Leyland National, Bristol VR/ECW double-deckers, and Leyland Olympians, the latter to replace the VRs, at least in part.

### LT Tendered Routes

  20  Walthamstow-Debden (daily) from 24.5.86 (partly tendered by Essex County Council)
 167  Ilford-Debden (daily) from 24.5.86
 193  Romford-Emerson Park (Mon-Sat) from 13.7.85
 235  Leytonstone station-Woodford Wells (schooldays only) from 6.3.89
 275  Walthamstow-Barkingside (daily) from 24.5.86
 307  Brimsdown station-Arkley (daily) from 27.9.86
 359  Holloway/Manor House-Waltham Cross/Hammond Street (daily) from 21.1.87 (former London Country North East from 25.10.86)
 379  Chingford station-Yardley Lane Estate (daily) from 5.3.89 (originally London Buses as 179A from 24.5.87, second contract by Grey Green from 17.10.87)
W9   Enfield-Muswell Hill Broadway (daily) from 13.7.85
W13  Leytonstone station-Woodford Wells (daily) from 4.3.89
W14  Leytonstone station-Claybury Hospital (daily) from 4.3.89 (formerly route 206, from 24.5.86)

A number of contracts will be lost during 3.92: 20/167/235/275 (to Grey Green) and W14 (to County). However, the W11/W12 will be added during 11.91.

Left:
Four all-Leyland Olympians were delivered for Thamesway London service in late 1990, including 1003 at Barnet Church on an eastbound 307 journey when new.
J. Waterhouse

Top:
Prior to the arrival of the Olympians, the Bristol VR has been the Thamesway double-deck choice. No 3080 proceeds down High Road, Tottenham on Manor House-bound 359 in March 1991.   Kevin Lane

Above:
Leyland Nationals 1920 and 1826 are in new and former liveries at Walthamstow in March 1991.   Kevin Lane

# Transcity Link Ltd

*152 Maidstone Road, Ruxley Corner, Sidcup, Kent*

A newcomer to LT-tendered services, Transcity Link is probably a name little-known to many enthusiasts. However, prior to its award of the B15, the company had been very active in North Kent in coaching, private hire and contract work, etc, as well as other local service work for Kent County Council and two commercial routes in the Dartford area. Also noteworthy is the 492A Sidcup-Bexleyheath, operated by agreement with LT (and on which Travelcards are available). Minibuses and midibuses are the order of the day, with Talbot Pullmans, Mercedes 811Ds and, as back-up, Freight Rover Sherpas used on the stage services.

**LT Tendered Route**
B15 Welling Corner-Joydens Wood (Mon-Sat) from 19.1.91 (formerly Selkent/Bexleybus from 16.1.88)

Above:
*F814 VAC, one of the Transcity Talbot Pullman six-wheelers, pulls away from Welling corner, Upper Wickham Lane in February 1991.* Kevin Lane

# OTHER
# OPERATORS

# OTHER OPERATORS

The LT tendering process is now well under way, with independent operators solidly established, in some areas to the exclusion of almost all red buses. This is not the end of the matter, as there are still a number of other independent operators working well into the London area, but not as part of the LT network. Some are, admittedly, very peripheral and merely nip across the boundary to the nearest large shopping area, but they are nevertheless worthy of inclusion. The following list is comprehensive but not exhaustive, as services come and go, but it will give a very good idea of who works where.

Mention should perhaps first be made of those larger, usually ex-NBC, operators which work into the area on routes other than those under tender from LT. London & Country is active in the Sutton and Croydon areas, Kentish Bus, not unexpectedly, works from Kent. County Bus & Coach can be found in the Romford (as can Eastern National) and Waltham Cross areas, while London Country North West works into Harrow, Northwood, Uxbridge and Staines, the latter also host to Alder Valley.

The largest of the independents to work solely within London disappeared in November 1990, namely Docklands Transit, after some 20 months, apparently due for the most part to its inability to get travel cards accepted on its services. However, I suspect that its fleet of 70-plus identical Ford Transits will be missed by few enthusiasts! Similarly, a service from Crawley to Victoria along the route of London Buses 109 and London & Country 405 operated by the Panther Corporation using Leyland Nationals also ceased towards the end of 1990.

A route still operating within the LRT area is the 398 between Northolt and Ruislip station worked by Scorpio Coaches using mainly Leyland Nationals and with a former London Country Bristol LH/ECW as a reserve vehicle. Worked under an agreement with LT, the service started in November 1987.

Borehamwood-based BTS has already been encountered, as it operates LT-tendered services 114 and 292. However, several other routes are operated, including former London Country town services (on which Metroriders are used) and the 355 Borehamwood-St Albans, regular vehicles on which would appear to be former Kelvin Scottish Metrobuses.

Above:
*GMA 404N is one of Scorpio's Leyland Nationals to be found working on its route 398, where it is seen at Ruislip station. The LT-type roundel actually has 'Scorpio Coaches' across the bar.*   Kevin Lane

Previous page:
*Welwyn Hatfield Line Optare City Pacer E999 UYG pauses outside Potters Bar station on a 302 journey from Welwyn Garden City in January 1991.*   Kevin Lane

Above:
*The Sunday workings of route 500, Harlow-Romford are in the hands of Blue Triangle. This ex-London AEC Merlin is seen in St Edward's Way, Romford.*   C. R. Warren

During the summer of 1990, BTS also took over operation of Potters Bar local route PB1 from North Mymms Coaches, using one of its Metroriders. But this has subsequently been passed to Sovereign.

While at Potters Bar, mention should be made of Welwyn Hatfield Line, now part of Sovereign Bus & Coach but retaining its separate identity — indeed, two Leyland Nationals have been put into its colours, supplementing their midibuses. These work on an hourly circular from Welwyn Garden City (302), at Hatfield-Potters Bar-Hatfield circular (312, which runs only on Mondays, Wednesdays, Fridays and Saturdays and then only twice a day), and the 201, Essendon Community bus, on Thursday only.

Wests of Woodford Green, with a fleet of mainly ex-NBC Leyland Nationals and new Metroriders, operates in the Loughton, Epping and Chingford areas. Services include the daily 201 Ongar-Epping-Loughton, 214/215 Debden circular, again daily (all run under contract to Essex County Council), 249 Loughton-South Woodford and the 531/532 Debden-Chingford, the latter services running Mondays to Saturdays only.

A number of Essex-based independents are of interest to us here: Blue Triangle, which also runs a sightseeing tour in central London, operates a couple of services, the 265 Romford station-Bulphan, Mondays to Saturdays, using Leyland Nationals, and the 500 Romford Market-Harlow, Sundays and Bank Holidays. Blue Triangle is well known for its fleet of former London Transport vehicles, including Routemasters, RTs and an RF, used on a variety of services such as contract, private hire and promotional work. Romford is the focus for other operators, such as District Bus of Wickford which has the 271-274 Basildon/Laindon-Romford on various days of the week; Jackson's Minicoaches of Bicknacre has a limited-stop journey between South Woodham and Romford on Wednesdays only, and Bonners Coaches of Ongar runs two return journeys between Epping and Romford on Saturdays. Finally, Bordercoach of Thundersley reaches Romford from Cheshunt on Wednesdays and Saturdays, and from only Waltham Cross on Fridays also.

Other services include: Golden Boy, Hoddesdon, with its 393 Hoddesdon/Harlow-Ongar service; the 209 Lambourne End/Abridge-Loughton on Wednesdays and Fridays worked by Vantage Coach Hire of Romford; RS Express Travel, Brentwood service 381, Toothill-Epping-Harlow, on Mondays to Fridays only; and Ongar Coaches' 217 (a Thursdays-only journey between Blake Hall and Ongar) and the 394 (Hastingwood-Epping on Mondays only).

Top:
*Five Plaxton-bodied Bedford YMTs are among the Epsom Buses fleet. D602 RGJ here enters Croydon on a 598 from Epsom in April 1990.   Kevin Lane*

Above:
*An Ashford Luxury Coaches ex-NCP Gatwick Leyland National 2, OGN 879Y, stands in Coleridge Crescent, terminus of the 305 from Staines to Poyle. The LT bus stop flag would seem superfluous.   Kevin Lane*

Below:

*Finally, back in central London, look out for the Victoria Shuttle between the railway and coach stations. Picking up in Buckingham Palace Road is D85 DOT, a Mercedes-Benz 709D, being passed by a London General OV class Optare City Pacer on a C1 duty.*

Kevin Lane

In southeast London, Transcity Link runs midibuses on its 492A Bexleyheath-Sidcup-Swanley service which runs from Monday to Friday only, although the company has recently become involved with LT tendering having acquired the B15 Welling-Joydens Wood.

Moving into Surrey, a prominent and long-established operator is Epsom Coaches, which began local bus work as Epsom Buses from 1986. Over a dozen routes are operated, several of which enter the LT area: these include the 3, Epsom-Worcester Park (Monday to Saturday); X5, Epsom to Kingston (Saturdays only); 8, Epsom to Chessington (Monday to Saturday); 293, Epsom-Morden (one morning journey and evenings); 508, Epsom-Sutton (Sundays and Bank Holidays); and 598, Epsom-West Croydon (Monday to Saturday). The fleet, based in Blenheim Road, Epsom, is a mixture of Plaxton bus-bodied Bedford YMTs, coach-bodied Leyland Leopards and Mercedes-Benz 709D and L608D midibuses.

East Surrey Buses, South Godstone, rubs shoulders with Epsom Buses at one or two places in the Croydon area. The two routes that concern us here are the 301, Croydon-Clockhouse Farm and 363, Coulsdon-Clockhouse Farm. The fleet is mainly Bedford, with Plaxton, Willowbrook and Duple bodies, while more recent deliveries have been Optare StarRiders and an Optare Metrorider.

Turning to the southwestern edge of the LT area, two operators can be found at Staines: Tellings-Golden Miller's 606 goes to Stanwell Moor, a Monday to Saturday operation with a Caetano-bodied Volvo B10M bus as the regular performer, and there is Ashford Luxury Coaches with a none-too-frequent 305 out to Poyle, using a Leyland National 2 from National Car Parks, Gatwick. This is, again, a Monday to Saturday service. Tellings-Golden Miller is now also involved in LT tender work.

Finally, Armchair, Brentford chips in with its 555, Chertsey-Heathrow Airport and 556/7, Weybridge/Walton-Heathrow Airport, usually worked by Leyland Swift/Wadham Stringer buses but sometimes by a Mercedes midibus or a coach of some sort. There is also the 601, Whiteley-Hampton Court-Kingston, which uses a Reeve-Burgess-bodied Mercedes-Benz 811D.

Thus there is more to London than meets the eye! Details of the actual services are not always easy to obtain, but some information about this is given in the section on ticketing and timetables.

# Coaching in the Capital

London has been a focal point for coach services since the early days of the industry. Offering a cheaper, if slower, alternative to the train (as it is today), many operators offered a service to the capital. An early problem was the lack of terminal facilities, with coaches picking up and setting down all over the place, which pleased the Metropolitan Police no end! A partial solution was the opening of Lupus Street coach station by London Coastal Coaches Ltd, in 1928. However, this site soon became overcrowded and congested, despite many operators still terminating elsewhere in the capital. The next solution of London Coastal Coaches is still with us, the coach station at Victoria which opened in 1932.

## Expresses

The National Express network, together with the associated Caledonian Express operations is the major coaching presence in London, with most services still using Victoria. As can be imagined, virtually any coach operator can turn up on some service or other, particularly during the summer, both on long-distance and more regular, shorter-haul routes.

There are several established routes out of London, depending on whether additional pick-ups are made. Many services to Scotland do not stop again in London, heading straight for the M1 motorway via Finchley Road and Hendon Way, while coaches for the East Midlands, Lancashire, Yorkshire and the North East may pick up at Marble Arch and/or Golders Green on the way to the motorway. Heading out west to South Wales and the West Country, many services call at Earls Court and Heathrow Airport, with those to the south coast travelling either through Elephant & Castle, New Cross and Lewisham or Stockwell, Streatham and Thornton Heath. Services to East Anglia generally leave London via Aldgate and Stratford.

## Other Termini

National Express and Victoria are by no means the end of the story, however. The deregulation of the coaching industry saw many new initiatives, a considerable number of which foundered (remember British Coachways?), although there are still many smaller operators working regularly into London to termini other than Victoria. Unfortunately, some of these are advertised only for the benefit of passengers travelling to London, so it is difficult to find out about them from the London end.

There is a small coach station in Wilton Road attached to the bus garage, in Victoria, and this is used by several services, including the London Liner operations of West Midlands Travel with a roughly two-hourly service to Birmingham, running daily, and Bere Regis Coaches, with a daily run from Bridport and Weymouth. Wilton Road is also used by London Coaches for its commuter routes, as described below.

## King's Cross

Since before the war there has been a terminus of some sort for coaches at King's Cross, and many may remember the windswept premises on the site of St Pancras goods depot which disappeared during the 1980s under the new British Library. Today, some coach services terminate in Pancras Road, between St Pancras and King's Cross railway stations, including Excelsior Coachways service from Poole and Bournemouth.

## Marylebone

A short distance to the west is another long-established terminal point, that at Marylebone station, for many years visited by United Counties, and still used by the current operator under the Stagecoach banner, with services to Corby and Kettering.

*bove:*
*e Finchley Road is an excellent place to see coaches entering and leaving London.*
*idland Red Coaches MCW Metroliner 1502 is showing both 550 and 555 service numbers*
*s it heads into central London. Following are two Green Line coaches and a pair of London*
*uses Metrobuses.   Kevin Lane*

*elow:*
*Dover-bound National Express working passes Lewisham in July 1990, with East Kent*
*CW-bodied Leyland Leopard 8829 in charge.   Kevin Lane*

# OTHER OPERATORS

### The Limited-Stop Network

For many years the main limited-stop network in and around London was provided by Lon-don Transport and subsequently London Country Bus Services, in the guise of Green Line. This, once comprehensive limited stop network has now all but disappeared, with route either abandoned, taken over by other operators or integrated into other services. Som remnants survive, Victoria, Eccleston Place, being the traditional terminus. Others such Luton & District's 757 from Luton and Luton Airport, a former Green Line route, use near Buckingham Palace Road.

Two former municipal operators are a familiar sight in London, Southend Transport a Reading Transport. Both offer X1 numbered services, as it was originally a joint serv between the two towns, although the route was severed in 1982. Today, Southend ru coaches which generally terminate at Hyde Park Corner — with a few continuing on Heathrow Airport — but has some peak journeys reaching only Embankment. Reading the other hand uses double-deckers through to Aldgate on its service.

### Commuting Coaches

So much for express and limited-stop services, but this leaves another area of operatio commuter coaching. To some degree these overlap with more normal, all-day, services, b many dedicated commuter services run during the week. The very nature of the operatio inward during the rush-hour and back home in the evening, leads them to be unseen many casual visitors.

Providing transport for commuters is a specialised business, and several operators sta out in the field. Perhaps the greatest concentration of such services is from the Medw towns, Rochester, Chatham, Gillingham and Sittingbourne, and North Kent. Grey Gre runs a number of services in the 8XX number series from such places as Snodland, Stroo Meopham and High Halstow, arriving at Victoria, Bressenden Place at between 07.55 a 09.05, departing between 16.05 and 18.05, some travelling via the city. Another well kno name is The Kings Ferry, running in from the Gillingham area and arriving at Victoria Str between 06.58 and 09.34, returning between 15.47 and 18.32. Furthermore, Maidstone District also runs in from the area (as indeed it does during the day), under the Invictaw name, arriving at Wilton Road coach station. Yet another group of services is provided London Coaches from North Kent, Northfleet, New Ash Green, etc, again finishing up Wilton Road. Other areas also provide traffic for commuter coaches, but in smaller nu bers, due generally to better rail services north of the Thames: the fortunes of these pe hour operations seem closely tied with the quality of the competing rail service.

Left:
*United Counties uses a terminus at Marylebone station for its services to Kettering and Corby. Here a collection of Volvo and Tiger coaches gather in the rain, all wearing Stagecoach corporate livery.   Kevin Lane*

Top:
*Heathrow Airport is, of course, a magnet for coach operators. The Railair Link between the airport and Reading began back in 1967, and currently uses Hestair-Duple 425 coaches of The Bee Line (Berks Bucks Bus Co Ltd) on the service, such as 773 seen here at Terminal 4 in December 1990.   Kevin Lane*

Above:
*Reading Transport Leyland Olympian 85 was photographed at Hammersmith Butterwick on an Aldgate-Reading X1 journey in April 1990.   Kevin Lane*

Above:
*Southend Transport has a significant commuter network between London and the Southend area. A quartet of coaches lines up on layover before commencing X10 workings at Aldgate, together with a Kentish Bus Leyland National on a 42, a tendered route since lost.*
Kevin Lane

Below:
*Grey Green is also very active in the commuter business. This Plaxton-bodied Volvo B10M is waiting in Bressenden Place to work the 805 16.30 departure to Frindsbury.* Kevin Lane

# Sightseeing Buses & Tourist Coaches

You cannot go very far in central London without coming across a sightseeing bus or a coach-load of tourists eager to take in the delights of the capital, even in the depths of winter. The vehicles are many and various, ranging from the dedicated open-top double-decker to a high-specification luxury coach complete with a commentary, the latter of course usually carrying many visitors from overseas.

**Original London Transport Sightseeing Tour**

Perhaps the highest profile is that of London Coaches' Original London Transport Sightseeing Tour, with, to quote an American tourist with whom I struck up a conversation, 'a good old fashioned red London bus' — in effect several varieties of Routemaster, of both open and closed top, reflecting the all-year nature of the service. The standard tour takes around 90min, departing from Victoria, Piccadilly Circus, Baker Street and Marble Arch, subsequently passing all the expected sights: the Tower of London, Tower Bridge, Big Ben, the Houses of Parliament, St Paul's Cathedral, Fleet Street and so on. Leaflets are available at information centres throughout London and the service operates every day except for Christmas Day. The 1991 adult price is £8.00 (£7.00 in advance). Apart from the tourist angle, open-top buses are a good way to take some out-of-the-ordinary pictures of other buses! London Coaches also operates a number of more up-market tours using its fleet of coaches, not only within London but throughout the country and even day trips to France.

A spin off, which started on 17 August 1991, is London Plus, using Routemasters (open-top ERMs in summer) in a special, predominantly cream livery. It too costs £8.00, but tickets are valid for two days and passengers can disembark and reboard at any of 30 stops between Tobacco Dock and the Royal Albert Hall. No commentary is given.

Above:
*A new tour for London Coaches in 1991, the London Plus Sightseeing Tour offers a hop on/hop off facility and with a ticket that is valid for two days, offers something different from the normal tours. ERM242 is seen in Victoria Street* Kevin Lane

Top:
*Former London DMS class Fleetlines predominate in the London Pride fleet, part of the Ensign Group. However, there is some relief, including this former Ribble (new to Blackburn) East Lancs-bodied Leyland Atlantean, seen at St Martins Place in October 1990.*
Kevin Lane

Above:
*A DMS at last! This particular example, formerly DMS447, heads north across Tower Bridge for London Sightseeing Tours Ltd, its closed top no doubt appreciated on a cold December afternoon.* Kevin Lane

Right:
*The other sightseeing operator to use Routemasters is Blue Triangle. RMO2118 is a former Northern General machine, caught by the camera on the Victoria Embankment.* Kevin Lane

## Other Services

The bus operating units too are involved in sightseeing work. London General, for example, ran a 'London by night' tour in 1990, again taking in a selection of the well known places of interest, many of which are floodlit after dark. This made an attractive and unusual tour, and was well priced at £3.00 for adults. Leaside, as mentioned under that heading, runs Leisure Bus 333 from Mile End to Waltham Abbey on summer Sundays and Bank Holidays, with London Northern running a connecting service around the Lee Valley Park as route 318. Furthermore, there are other initiatives, such as the tour of the Christmas lights run by East London in 1990. Some normal routes are also being promoted with the tourist in mind, London General for example having issued a leaflet extolling the virtues of its route 11, Routemaster-worked off Victoria, which passes Mansion House, St Paul's Cathedral, Trafalgar Square, Parliament Square and Westminster Abbey on its way from Liverpool Street station to Shepherds Bush.

There are several other operators which offer a broadly similar itinerary to that of the OLST. London Pride, part of Ensignbus, operates a fleet consisting mainly of former London DMS class Daimler Fleetlines, although exceptions include Atlanteans from Ribble, Southdown and London Country North West, and the celebrated 'Megaliners', decapitated MCW Metroliners, new to Shamrock & Rambler but acquired from North Western. Another operator, the London Tour Company, was taken over by London Pride during 1990, although whether any of its mixed fleet, including Bristol VRs and ex-Salford Atlanteans, see duty in 1991 remains to be seen.

Another prolific DMS operator is London Cityrama, which has both open and closed-top varieties, although a few other types such as an ex-Trent Atlantean or an Optare-bodied Leyland Olympian may appear.

London Sightseeing Tours is another familiar sight, whose fleet is almost all — guess what? — yet more DMSs! Certainly the type can be regarded as a London sightseeing standard. The trouble is that many buses carry all-over adverts and as such are not easily identified at a first glance. For a more luxurious tour, Harrods provides a pair of Neoplan Skyliners in the company's house colours, a sort of olive green and gold.

Finally, and perhaps most interestingly, Blue Triangle operates its own tour from Easter until October, departing from Whitehall (opposite the Cenotaph) with a variety of interesting vehicles, and a newcomer in 1991, The Big Bus Company, uses an ex-East Kent full-front AEC Regent V open-topper and DMSs, all in a maroon and cream colour scheme derived from traditional East Kent livery.

# OTHER OPERATORS

### Coach Tours

There are also a number of organised sightseeing tours using coaches, such as Frames Rickards which runs full and half-day tours around London using a fleet of burgundy and gold Volvo B10M Leyland Tiger coaches. Other tours are often part of a package holiday and can be seen unloading camera-toting tourists on such places as Westminster Bridge in some numbers during the summer months. Vehicles are often on hire to a particular tour company, making a lot of interest for the coaching enthusiast. A different kind of tour can be organised by the London Docklands Development Corporation, giving group tours of Docklands, either in a vehicle hired by the LDDC or using the customer's own coach.

### Overseas Visitors

An increasingly common sight in London these days is coaches from mainland Europe offering even more variety. French and German vehicles appear to dominate, but those from many countries, occasionally beyond Europe, seem to make their way to London, sometimes bringing an exotic chassis/bodywork combination. Coach parking is notoriously scarce in London, and therefore vehicles can turn up almost anywhere, even parked in side streets. Usually they can be found in numbers at places such as along the Embankment and at the Marble Arch end of Park Lane. There may also be a few at the coach park at the southern end of Vauxhall Bridge, while the obvious tourist centres may well produce a vehicle or two. However, when inspecting or photographing Continental vehicles, be prepared for inquisitive drivers (and passengers) — a selection of phrase books could come in handy!

Left:
*Harrods' olive green Neoplan Skyliner A122 RTL, one of two similar coaches new in 1983, goes about its business in Lambeth Palace Road.*   Kevin Lane

Top:
*Tourist coaches can be found at all the popular places at any time of the year. Outside St Paul's Cathedral in January 1991 were G650 LWF, an Ikarus-bodied Volvo B10M-60 of Swallow Luxury Coaches, Rainham, Essex, and RBC 705W, a Bedford YMT/Duple of Scotts Travel, Swanley, Kent.*   Kevin Lane

Above:
*Visitors from abroad tend to originate from either France or Germany, but as Eastern Europe becomes more closely linked with the West, coaches from the more far-flung countries are bound to increase. This Czechoslovak Karosa LC736 integral of CSAD Bratislava was pictured on the Victoria Embankment.*   Graham Wise

# Tickets and Timetables

For those wishing to make a day out of exploring London's buses, there are two types of tickets that fit the bill, both with their own merits.

### The One-Day Bus Pass
This pass is available from most bus garages and selected newsagents and can be bought in several forms, depending on which zones are required. There are no time restrictions, but it cannot be used on N-prefixed night routes, nor in Zone 1, the central area.

### One-Day Travelcard
For much more freedom, a One-Day Travelcard is the ticket. It is available throughout all zones on not just the buses, but on the Underground and British Rail also, but not before 09.30 Monday to Friday. While trains may not be of interest to some bus enthusiasts, they are essential for longer journeys as bus travel can be excruciatingly slow, particularly in the central area. Restrictions are few: it cannot be used on Airbus or night routes, although it is valid on the Docklands Light Railway, good fun to travel on. A further advantage to this ticket is that its purchase can be combined with a day return ticket from Network SouthEast stations outside the LT area, thus saving the need to re-book in the capital.

The actual boundary within which one can travel with these tickets is roughly as follows: Elstree, Enfield, Loughton, Upminster, Crayford, Knockholt, Coulsdon, Cheam, Surbiton, Feltham, West Drayton, Uxbridge, West Ruislip, Northwood and Stanmore. This does not correspond with the LT bus network, as some routes pass way beyond the boundary (the 310A for example runs out to Hertford from Enfield). Thus several interesting centres unfortunately lie just out of reach, such as Dartford, Epsom and Potters Bar. The 1991 price for an adult One-Day Travelcard is £3.10, surely one of today's travel bargains.

There is also an all-day, all-zone Travelcard called LT Card. It is not valid on BR and it costs £5.50 (1991), but unlike the One-Day Travelcard can be used before 09.30 during the week. If you need to travel before 09.30, though, it could be cheaper to pay for a sinlge fare and buy a Travelcard later in the day . . . !

### Maps
Apart from a ticket, the other essential item is a London bus map, available free from travel centres, bus garages, etc, which should tell you most of what you need to know to get around, with the exception of service frequencies. These are detailed in the local bus guides (of which there are currently 36), which also include detailed street plans of important centres, even down to the position of shops (so if you need to know where the Swiss Cottage branch of Spud-U-Like is, then you need local bus guide No 8 . . .).

### Timetables
Timetables generally are not that essential, as the majority of routes tend to offer a high level of service, except for the more rural ones; and, in any case, information at bus stops is good.

For bus services entering from outside the LT area, one usually has to consult the relevant county council timetable book. Essex County Council, for instance, produces two hefty volumes, which include peripheral routes around Romford, Loughton and Epping, while both Surrey and Hertfordshire have carried on the style of the old London Country timetables.

# WHERE TO
# GO;
# WHAT TO SEE

## Central London

It is difficult to know exactly where to start, when dealing with such a dense area of bus
activity. However, most visiting enthusiasts will at some time want to see, photograph and
ride on a Routemaster. Despite the fact that the type is becoming common in certain other
areas of the country, there is nothing like the 'real thing'.

### Routemaster

The Routemaster is still a familiar beast in central London, there being (1991) over 900 of
the type in stock, including sightseeing vehicles, and it is only when you travel out to many
of the 'one-person-operated' suburbs that you realise that so many have been withdrawn in
the past. The list of routes on which Routemasters are still scheduled is currently standing
at 25: 2B, 3, 6, 7, 8, 9, 10, 11, 12, 13, 14, 15, 15B, X15, 19, 22, 36, 36A, 36B, 38, 73, 88, 94,
137 and 159. Routemasters appear on these on Mondays to Saturdays only, although the
sightseeing operations are daily.

A perusal of the bus map will soon reveal that all of the above routes either start from, or
pass through, central London, with half of them going via Oxford Circus. As such, the type
works in much of the area, and one will come across them sooner or later! Good concentrations of Routemasters are found from Marble Arch, along Oxford Street and beyond to Hol-
born Circus, Bank and King's Cross; south from Marble Arch through Hyde Park Corner to
Victoria and on to Vauxhall; Knightsbridge, Piccadilly Circus, Trafalgar Square, Strand,
along Fleet Street to St Paul's — the list goes on. Many of the traditional tourist areas have
the added attraction of passing Routemasters on service or on sightseeing duties, handy if
you have the family with you. Make sure also that you manage actually to ride on a
Routemaster, although expect to be caught up in traffic before you get very far. (At least
with a rear-loader you are able to hop on and off when stuck in traffic jams.)

Above:

*A few minutes from Parliament Square is Parliament Street, leading into Whitehall. It is a
very busy thoroughfare for buses, more so when the tourist season gets underway. RM1804
passes the Cenotaph on a 3 from Crystal Palace.*   Kevin Lane

Previous page:

*St Paul's Cathedral looms in the background as RM1725 proceeds down Ludgate Hill on a
westbound 11 on a damp January morning in 1991.*   Kevin Lane

*Above:*
*At the north end of Whitehall is Trafalgar Square and the Strand. DMS 2355 stands opposite Charing Cross station (the cross itself unfortunately camouflaged by the surrounding buildings) near to the end of an Aldwych-bound 170.* Kevin Lane

## The Independent Way

Another subject which will be high on the visiting enthusiast's 'shopping list' will be independent operators working LT-tendered services. In the early days, these were very much suburban affairs, but have gradually crept towards central London, with the result that there are quite a few today. Grey Green Volvo Citybuses appear on the 24, which passes Westminster, Trafalgar Square and Tottenham Court Road, and the 168 which can be seen at Euston and Waterloo. Kentish Bus puts on a good show with Olympians on the 22A, 22B and the 55, all of which can be seen in Hackney, east London, but originate at London Bridge, Piccadilly Circus and Tottenham Court Road respectively. The 42, Aldgate-Camberwell is also operated, using Leyland Nationals or Metroriders. R&I Coaches also penetrates to the central area, reaching King's Cross with its C12 from Finchley Road with Dennis Darts.

London & Country has made a colourful entry into the central area, now working the 78 Forest Hill-Shoreditch and 176 Oxford Circus-Penge with East Lancs-bodied Volvo Citybuses. On the edge of the central area could be included London Buslines' C4 at Chelsea Harbour, worked with Mercedes midibuses.

## Central Centres

Other than the Routemasters, most other classes of London Buses' vehicles can be found working in the central area. It may be useful therefore to review some of the more popular centres:

*Oxford Circus*

This is a very busy junction with Regent Street, with Routemasters in abundance on routes 3, 6, 7, 8, 10, 12, 13, 15, 15B, X15, 73, 88, 137 and 159, other routes using Metrobuses, Titans and Olympians, with Leyland National 2s on Red Arrow 503 and Optares on route C2. The 176 is in the hands of London & Country.

# WHERE TO GO, WHAT TO SEE

*Trafalgar Square*

Again, there are many Routemasters around on the 3, 6, 9, 11, 12, 13, 15, 15B, X15, 88 an 159, but among the modern types can be added the DMS. The London & Country 176 als comes this way, as does Grey Green's 24. Trafalgar Square is also a regular haunt of th sightseeing buses, while a short walk along the Strand to Aldwych will net Red Arrow route 501/502/505/513.

*Bank*

Routemaster activity can be found on the 6, 8, 9, 11, 15B and, at the time of writing, X1 while Leyland Titans are also around in large numbers, with Metrobuses and Olympians les so. The 133 adds some more variety with VC class Volvo Citybuses, as does Red Arro route 501. Finally, look out for Kentish Bus Olympians on the 22B.

*Aldgate*

Just down the road from Bank, Aldgate has a small bus station opposite the Undergroun station, used mainly by London Buses on terminating services, and by National Express Southend Transport and Reading Transport, the latter two on their X1 limited-stop services In adjacent Aldgate High Street, delights include midibus route 100, Kentish Bus 42 fo Camberwell Green, and Routemasters yet again, this time just on the 15/15B/X15. Londo & Country also puts in an appearance on the 78.

*Westminster*

One for all the family! The area around Parliament Square, including Westminster Bridge Victoria Embankment and Whitehall, is certainly worth investigating. There is a concentra tion of tourist sights, including Big Ben, the Houses of Parliament, Westminster Abbey, an Horse Guards Parade. Needless to say, sightseeing buses abound, even in winter, whil Victoria Embankment is a popular parking place for visiting coaches. A good mix of buse can be seen: Routemasters on the 3, 11, 12, 88 and 159, with Titans, Olympians Metrobuses and DMSs also in evidence, and some early-morning weekday extensions o the 196 beyond Kennington will bring VC class Volvo Citybuses, too. Minibus route C1 wi contribute Optare Metroriders. Independent interest is maintained by Grey Green Volv Citybuses on the 24. There are many good photographic locations: Big Ben, for example, i well photographed with buses from Broad Sanctuary and from the southern end of West minster Bridge, while the Cenotaph and the Houses of Parliament, too, are worth includin in photographs.

*Victoria*

It is easy for a regular visitor to London, like myself, to get dismissive about the over-familia places such as Victoria, but it really is a 'must', even if you have time to go nowhere else. circular tour can be recommended, starting at the bus station outside the main railway sta tion. Services here use either the under-cover bus station or adjacent Terminus Place departing vehicles pointing east. The usual variety of types are represented, including Routemasters, of course, and Red Arrow routes 507 and 510. A short walk down Wilto Road, along which Grey Green's 24 runs, brings us to the coach station of the same name adjacent to Gillingham Street London General garage. This is the departure point for certai commuter services, including those operated by London Coaches, and the London Line services to Birmingham, with West Midlands Travel. Heading up Gillingham Street and pas the garage entrance (where there is always something to see within, including visiting coaches such as those off the London Liner and the Clipper service from Newcastle), tur right on to Eccleston Bridge, terminus of many Green Line routes. How many pictures o buses have been taken in front of Bishop & Sons, Furniture Depositories, I wonder?

Over Buckingham Palace Road and left into Eccleston Place: on the right is the forme Samuelsons garage, now used as a setting-down point for some express services, easin the congestion in the coach station over the road. Also here is a pick-up point for the Victo ria Shuttle, a minibus service to and from the railway station.

Above:
Victoria is a 'must' for any visitor to London; coaches terminate at several points in the area. This Busways (Armstrong Galley) Scania is loading in Wilton Road for Newcastle in January 1991. Kevin Lane

Below:
The London General Victoria garage is in Gillingham Street (hence the GM garage code) and also plays host to coaches using Wilton Road coach station. Accompanying RM2161 is West Midlands Travel MCW Metroliner 400GT on London Liner duties from Birmingham. Kevin Lane

Above:
*The London Transport Museum is in Covent Garden: besides the delights within, it is sometimes the venue for special events. Ian Allan Ltd held a special event on 11 March 1989, and included a bus service to and from Aldwych Underground station. Performers included these two preserved buses, Southampton Guy Arab 71 and Aldershot & District Dennis Lance 145.* Kevin Lane

The great edifice of the coach station looms opposite, services departing either into Elizabeth Street or Ebury Street, arriving via Semley Place. All coaching life is found here at some time or other, and at busy times the passengers milling around the hordes of coaches is a fascinating spectacle, perhaps best observed from the adjacent multi-storey car park. If on the ground, be careful where you wander or risk the wrath of the roving inspectors! Back into Buckingham Palace Road, turn left and it is back to the railway station again. Also noteworthy are the various sightseeing buses departing from nearby Grosvenor Gardens (the Original London Sightseeing Tour leaves from Victoria Street) and commuter coaches to the Medway towns at peak periods in Bressenden Place.

A couple of options from Victoria are to Vauxhall, where there is a coach park just over the bridge, or to Pimlico, terminus of the Grey Green 24, beside the Thames in Grosvenor Road.

*Thames bridges*
There are a number of bridges over the Thames which make an interesting location for bus pictures. Tower Bridge is possibly the most interesting and is crossed by Kentish Bus 42, London & Country 78, the Carelink minibus and any number of sightseeing buses.

Space precludes a description of all parts of the central area, but most other areas will bear fruit — just take a look at the central area bus map to see where the busiest places are. Mention should finally be made of the London Transport Museum at Covent Garden, open daily between 10.00 and 18.00.

# North London

North London is an area well served by the Underground which can be used to some advantage. We will begin at Camden, a focal point for many routes, including Grey Green's 24 and 168: Camden Lock is a good place to photograph both. (The area around Camden Town Underground station [Northern Line] is rather congested, thwarting many a promising bus photograph.) Minibus route C2 passes through from Regent Street to Parliament Hill Fields, some short workings terminating at the station. The one-way systems in the vicinity can make life confusing, so the relevant local bus guide (No 8) would be useful.

North of Camden, try Archway, another busy centre with independent activity from R&I Tours on the C11/12 and Grey Green on the 210, the latter continuing up Highgate Hill to Highgate Village and on across Hampstead Heath to Golders Green — an attractive journey.

### Finchley

Following the Northern Line from Archway and through Highgate, the 263 with its Scanias will be encountered at East Finchley, while Finchley Central is more interesting with RMLs passing on the 13 and Armchair Olympians on the 260, although everything else is likely to be a Metrobus. A 13/26/82 or 260 will take you to Golders Green, dealt with in the north-west section, while in the other direction, Ballards Lane will take you to North Finchley, Tally Ho! Corner, terminus also of the Grey Green 125 to Winchmore Hill/Enfield. Finchley garage, opened as a tram depot in 1905, can be glimpsed just off Ballards Lane at its northern end.

To return a minute to Finchley Central, the single-track Mill Hill East branch will give access via the 221/240 to the delights of Edgware, again covered in detail in the northwest section.

Above:
*North Finchley, Tally Ho! Corner, in July 1990. RML2345 is loading on the right, while RML2663 has just arrived, both buses working the 13 route. Leaside M336 sits on layover from a 221.*  Kevin Lane

Above:
*Barnet Church dominates the town centre and is prominent in this view of an Atlas Bus Leyland Olympian passing on a westbound 107 in December 1990.* Kevin Lane

Right:
*Two non-standard types stand outside Potters Bar garage: Volvo Ailsa V3, the one built with a rear exit, and Metrobus M1448, acquired from Yorkshire Rider in 1987.* Kevin Lane

### North to Barnet

North from Finchley, the road approximately follows the Northern Line through Whetstone to Barnet. Activity is centred around Barnet Hill and Barnet Church. London Northern uses second-hand Metrobuses as well as Scanias in the area, and look out also for a Metrorider on the tendered 384, terminating at the Spires Shopping Centre in the High Street. Thamesway, using Leyland Olympians and Bristol VRs, works from Arkley, Wood Street east to Brimsdown on the 307, while Atlas Bus Olympians can be found on the 107, which westbound will pass another worthwhile stopping-off point, Borehamwood.

An operator soon to be seen in the town is BTS, whose depot is next to the railway station. It works local town routes, inherited from London Country North West, with new Metroriders, and the tendered 292 on which its Alexander-bodied Scanias are likely to be seen. Also passing along the main street, Shenley Road, is a Hertfordshire County Council route, the 355, which runs hourly to St Albans, with ex-Kelvin Scottish Metrobuses seemingly common. Other services include Sovereign and Luton & District, which together with BTS work the 357/358 to Harpenden at various times; and London Country North West on the 306/309 from Garston, the former including Lucketts of Watford, on some journeys. If continuing on the 107 towards Queensbury, Elstree Village is attractive, while nearby the road passes over the M1 motorway, for pictures of coaches, etc.

### Potters Bar

Back at Barnet, it is a short journey, to Potters Bar, where London Northern has a garage. There are two areas of interest here, at the railway station and the aforementioned London Northern garage. At the former there is a sort of bus station, with London Northern 84 and 242 as well as Sovereign on local services PB1/PB3 formerly operated by North Mymms Coaches (and London Buses and BTS prior to that). Grey Green terminates on its tendered 313 from Chingford, and also calling at Welwyn-Hatfield Line, now part of Sovereign, on a couple of routes. A walk of five or 10min along The Walk, along which the half-hourly PB1 runs, and a right turn into the High Street, will bring you to Potters Bar garage, outside which the PB1 and 234/263 terminate. Another service to note, running along the southern end of town along Mutton Lane, is another Grey Green route, the 298 from Turnpike Lane to South Mimms, although this is due to pass to Ensign Citybus during 2.92.

### Cockfosters and Southgate

East from Barnet, Cockfosters, the northern terminus of the Piccadilly Line, plays host to the 384 and Grey Green 298, pulling in opposite directions. Two stations down the line is Southgate, with its integral bus station. A number of services circulate, including Grey Green 298 again, as well as the 125, and Thamesway's W9, running to a 20min off-peak frequency between Enfield and Muswell Hill using Mercedes midibuses. The remaining daytime service is the Metrobus-operated 121. A recommended position for pictures is nearby island where an elderly signpost can be included in the photograph.

### Enfield

Enfield can be reached from Southgate via the 121 or the W9. There is a small bus station off Church Street which is used by some services, including County Bus 310/316/360 and 383, and Grey Green 125. Others use a variety of stops in Cecil Road, Church Street and The Town. Again, the local bus guide, in this case No 12, should be consulted. Leaside Buses has a garage in Enfield — or more accurately in Ponders End — in Southbury Road near to the railway station (Southbury), rebuilt in 1984 from that built originally in 1927. The current allocation is exclusively Metrobus.

Below:
*The cluster of signposts near to Southgate station is illustrated here, and being passed by Grey Green Metrobus 453 (acquired from South Yorkshire in 1988) heading for Turnpike Lane on a 298.* Kevin Lane

Above:

*Tottenham High Cross, over the road from Tottenham garage, provides a useful background to Leaside Metrobus M1233, albeit surrounded by the ugly clutter of late 20th century street furniture.*   Kevin Lane

## Waltham Cross

North from Ponders End is the Travelcard border town of Waltham Cross, largely a mixture of London Buses and County Bus & Coach, although Thamesway works the 359, an LT-tendered route between Hammond Street/Waltham Cross and Holloway, Wests the infrequent 252 to Chingford, and Bordacoach on its route 8, a three-day a week shopping facility to Romford.

## A Journey to Waltham

Waltham Cross is easily reached from Liverpool Street by train, but a more leisurely way would be a bus journey along the A1010 and A10 down to the City, running more or less in a straight line from north to south. There is a great concentration of services all the way along, with plenty to see. At Edmonton Green there is a busy bus station with walkways to make photography easy; while further south, Tottenham garage is just off the High Road in Philip Lane, currently with an allocation of RMLs and Metrobuses, the former for route 73 to Victoria. A little further on in Rookwood Road, at the end of Egerton Road, off Stamford Hill High Road, is Stamford Hill garage, a building that has origins going back to 1907 when it was opened for trams — nothing so exotic these days, only Metrobuses. At the end of Stamford Hill High Road is the depot of Grey Green, often with something of interest on the forecourt. The road continues through Dalston, past the long-established photography suppliers, Frank Martin (where regular forays were once made on resurrected RCLs) and through Shoreditch to Liverpool Street, where the train would have got you rather quicker!

# East London

The area to the east of London has seen a fair amount of the tendering process over th past few years, with Grey Green, Ensign and Thamesway all providing a major contributio to the local bus network.

**Stratford Variety**
A good start can be made at Stratford, easily reached by either the Underground or Britis Rail from Liverpool Street. It has a gloomy bus station sandwiched between the railway sta tion and the shopping centre, and services include Grey Green 173 out to Becontree Heat (not on Sundays), and midibus route S2, an East London working off Bow. Everything else Leyland Titan worked, something that applies to most of London Buses' double-deck ope ation in East London. It is worthwhile walking to the top of the multi-storey car park on to of the bus station to photograph vehicles arriving, although as these arrive from the south the sun may prove a problem. Stratford is a stopping off point for National Express coache travelling to and from East Anglia, calling just to the north of the bus station exit. Othe activity takes place in the Broadway, including another LT contract route, the 108, operate by Boro'line using Leyland Lynxes.

Stratford is on the end of the northern branch of the Docklands Light Railway, allowing quick access to Docklands. The DLR does not currently run at weekends or during th evenings, and at such times a replacement bus service is provided by a Titan from Wes Ham garage.

**Docklands Operations**
Docklands itself, ever akin to a massive building site, has not too much variety, bus-wise Since the demise of the Docklands Minibus network, almost all services are worked by Eas London, and with Titans at that. A notable exception is the D1 Docklands Express, from Waterloo to the Isle of Dogs, Harbour Exchange Square, operated by London Forest usin dedicated Titans. The one non-London Bus route on the Isle of Dogs is the P14, worked b Kentish Bus Metroriders. Perhaps more interest can be found along the Commercial Roa and East India Dock Road, running across the top of the Isle of Dogs and into the City Among the services to traverse this traffic-choked route into town are the RMC-worked X1 (which runs non-stop between Poplar and St Katharine's Dock, and to attain this as muc as possible diverts off the route in places, though is due to be converted to one-perso operation in November 1991), the RML-worked 5, Green Line 723 and Southend Transpor services. While on the Docklands Light Railway, Bow garage is in Fairfield Road, round th corner from Bow Church station. This garage has an attractive frontage, dating fror 1908/10 and currently housing RMLs (for the 8), Titans and midibuses. The other East Lon don garage to use the Routemaster is Upton Park, responsible for the 15 group, includin the X15. Situated in Redclyffe Road, it is a short walk from Upton Park Underground statio There is also a garage in nearby West Ham, now all Titan, in Greengate Street, and th nearest station is Plaistow.

Above right:
*Home-going crowds on a Saturday afternoon at Stratford bus station: Grey Green Scania/East Lancs 114 leaves on a 173 to Becontree Heath.* Kevin Lane

Right:
*Island Gardens is on the tip of the Isle of Dogs and is the southern terminus of the Docklands Light Railway. The Kentish Bus Metrorider is on a P14 route working, while the East London Titan is on a Mile End-bound D7.* Kevin Lane

Top:
*Outside Barking railway station, Ensign 465, a former Ribble and Plymouth Atlantean, passes on a 62A in May 1990.* Kevin Lane

Above:
*Romford railway station is the scene for County Bus Atlantean AN247 running out to Grays in October 1990. The bus is carrying Thameside fleetnames, the local identity for the Grays area.* Kevin Lane

Right:
*There are plenty of buses in Western Road, Romford in this view; Ensignbus 213, a former London DMS, is on non-tendered route 449, and has other Ensign buses, an Atlantean and an Olympian, and two East London Titans, for company.* Kevin Lane

## arking to Ilford

he next large centre is Barking, with most of the activity taking place near the railway sta-
on, along East Street, London Road and Ripple Road. Most of the London Buses to be
ound are East London Titans working off Barking garage (itself in Longbridge Road; turn
ft out of the station and keep on going). Independent interest is maintained by Ensign
ouble-deckers on the 62/62A (though soon to pass to East London) and Grey Green on the
79.

To the north of Barking is Ilford, where London Buses and Titans are again much in evi-
ence. Again, outside the station is as good a place as any to see buses: Grey Green
asses this way on route 179, as does Thamesway on the 167, scheduled for Leyland
ationals, the latter to become a Grey Green route also in March 1992.

## perators in Romford

nd so to Romford, probably with a greater variety of operators than anywhere else in Lon-
on, on local bus services at least. Starting at the station, there is a small bus station adjac-
nt, with some attractive reproduction street lamps, and even finials on the 'no entry' signs!
he traffic avoids the town centre by taking the ring road to the other side, not too good for
hotographs but fine if you want to 'collect' operators. The area around the station is quite
usy, with London Buses, Ensign, Grey Green, County and Thamesway all in evidence.
Continuing around the ring road to St Edward's Way, more operators will be found, includ-
ig Eastern National, and a host of small independents, most of which are less than regular,
ind which are described in detail under 'other operators'. One to look out for, however, is
he 265 from Bulphan/West Horndon, operated by Blue Triangle using Leyland Nationals. It
ontinues through to Romford station and can also be photographed at Gidea Park, the
ext station on from Romford. Romford East London garage is in North Street and is
nother Leyland Titan stronghold. Included in its number are the first 41 and T1128, one of
hose acquired from West Midlands, and having coach seating. Southeast from Romford is
Jpminster, eastern end of the District Line, with local services in the hands of County and
Ensign, while District Bus also works in from the Basildon area, using midibuses.

# WHERE TO GO, WHAT TO SEE

### Loughton Independents

Moving now to the northwest, and to the northern extent of the Travelcard area on the Cen tral Line, is Loughton, once with a London Transport garage and now the preserve of inde pendents, with the exception of night route N96, Titan-worked from Leyton. Thameswa and County work the 20 and 250 respectively, while the other services are in the care  Wests Coaches, with a varied fleet including Metroriders, Leyland Nationals and a DA Optare Delta. Almost all services call at the Underground station and can be followed up  to the High Road and the town centre. More variety will previal when Grey Green takes ove on the 20.

### Chingford

Wests Coaches 531/532 provide a direct link with Chingford, albeit not part of the LT ne work. Yet another town where the buses terminate at the railway station, Chingford see several operators calling at the semi-circular bus station. Apart from Wests, there is Gre Green on both the 179 and 313, Thamesway on the 379 with midibuses, and County on a out-of-town route, the 505 Walthamstow-Harlow. London Buses also has several routes, a inevitably worked by Leyland Titans.

Chingford enjoys a quick and frequent rail service to Liverpool Street, trains runnin through Walthamstow Central. As well as an interchange with the Underground (Victori Line), Walthamstow also boasts a large bus station over the road. London Buses is mostl Titan, but Metrobuses appear on the 34 and there are also several Metrorider-worke routes. Furthermore, there is Thamesway on the 20 and 275 tendered routes and the lon 251 to Southend. County 505, which we encountered at Chingford, terminates here, to The loss of those contracts formerly worked by London Forest, largely to Ensign Citybus, i 11.91 will bring more variety still.

### Developments at Wanstead

Heading east again briefly, a recommended stop is at Wanstead, also on the Central Line Although not known previously as an exciting bus centre, it is quite interesting these days Passing along the A12 is the 66, County-worked using Leyland Lynxes, while the station the terminal point for Boro'line Maidstone's 108 from Lewisham, in practice in nearb Woodbine Place. Thamesway midibuses feature on the W12/W13 with County on the W14 while Thamesway's 251 to Southend, Olympian worked, also calls. Otherwise Titans are th red bus representative again.

### Last Stop: Hackney

One final place to recommend is Hackney, or more precisely, the area around Mare Stree and Hackney Central station. Immediately opposite the station, and set back off Mar Street, is London Forest's Clapton garage with a large allocation of Routemasters for the 3 and Metroriders for the 236 and W15. Buses passing outside include a number of Titan worked routes, Routemasters on the 38, midibuses on the 276 and W15 and the Leyland National-worked D6. However, perhaps the greatest impact is made by the Kentish Bu Olympians, to be seen in some numbers as they parade through on routes 22A/22B and 55 all high-frequency services.

Above:
*South meets east at Wanstead, as Boro'line Maidstone Leyland Lynx 801 arrives in Woodbine Place on a 108 from Lewisham, passing Thamesway Mercedes 0255 on a W14 working, in October 1990. The W14 passes to County during 3/92.* Kevin Lane

Below:
*South meets east at Hackney. Kentish Bus Olympians 'en masse' in Mare Street, by Hackney Central station. Bus 524 leads to others heading towards the city in March 1991.* Kevin Lane

# South East London

he first stopping-off point is Surrey Quays, easily reached by taking the East London Line
rom Whitechapel or the 188 from Euston and Waterloo. The shopping centre, focal point
or a number of services, was built over the old Canada Dock, part of the Surrey Commer-
ial Docks which closed over 20 years ago, although there are still reminders of its former
se, here and there. Buses serving the shops, which are over the road from the Under-
round station, include several midibus routes, Selkent 225, London Central P11/P13 and
Kentish Bus P14, as well as a couple of 'big bus' routes, bringing Titans and Olympians
lso.

The East London Line southwards will take you either to New Cross or New Cross Gate,
both situated on New Cross Road, a busy thoroughfare. New Cross Gate is the busier with
raffic entering Lewisham Way also, including plenty of Routemaster activity on the
6/36A/36B group of services. New Cross London Central garage is situated off the main
oad just west of New Cross Gate station, but activity is not easily seen as the building is
et back from the road. Current allocation is Titans and Olympians with Optare StarRiders
or the P3.

## Recommended

Lewisham is the next convenient place to call, ideally on a Routemaster on either a 36 or
36B (a 36A will take you south to Brockley Rise). There is a small bus station off the main
oad (not served by the 36/36B), which is used by services including Boro'line Maidstone on
he Lynx-operated 108, and Metrobus (of Orpington) route 261 on which a double-decker is
used. Lewisham High Street is quite photogenic and there is a clock tower worthy of inclusion in pictures. London Buses activity, RMs apart, is Titan and Olympian, with several
midibus routes for good measure. Recommended!

Lewisham High Street continues to Rushey Green and Catford, where the fare is much of
the same. Catford garage is in Bromley Road, quite a distance from Catford town centre;
indeed, the nearest station is Bellingham. Vehicles park on the frontage of the 1914 garage,
which is east-facing so is awkward for the sun in the afternoon. We are in Selkent territory

Above:
*A damp prospect at Surrey Quays with T1003 of Bromley heading for home on a 1 from
Trafalgar Square.* Kevin Lane

Top:
*A busy scene in Lewisham High Street in August 1990. As well as the two Leyland Titans, there is MC1, a Carlyle-bodied Mercedes-Benz that was formerly a demonstrator for the bodybuilder. While this remains unique at Catford, four more have been bought for use in Orpington.* Kevin Lane

Above:
*Bromley North station displaying its Southern Railway origins in October 1990, with a Metrobus Leyland Olympian and a Selkent Metrorider, MRL58, loading outside.* Kevin Lane

ow, and the allocation at Catford is either Leyland Titan or Routemaster for full-sized buses and Optare StarRiders, Wright-bodied Mercedes, and one each of the MC and MT class, Mercedes with Carlyle and Reeve-Burgess bodywork respectively. Midibuses carry a black and white cat motif on the sides by the front wheels. Another single representative at Catford is TPL4, a Plaxton-bodied Leyland Tiger coach.

## orth to South

nd so to Bromley. If you have arrived from Catford, it is convenient to begin at Bromley orth station and work your way down to Bromley South. The nicely restored Southern Railway frontage to the North station is a suitable backdrop to a variety of operators, including etrobus, Kentish Bus, London & Country and London Buses. There are a few good places r pictures in the vicinity of the station and down towards Market Square, but with the top d of the High Street now pedestrianised, buses skirt round via Kentish Way and Elmfield ay to regain it further down. The aforementioned independent activity comes this way, and past Bromley South station (which has a frequent service from London, a fast train service from Victoria taking only 16min). The bulk of services continue towards Bromley Common, where Selkent has its garage. Before this is reached there is a busy terminus at the nction with Crown Lane, where two Orpington area Roundabout routes terminate, the 1/R11, both midibus-operated with Dennis Darts.

The Selkent Bromley garage is in Hastings Road and was opened in 1924. It currently buses Titans, Dennis Darts, Leyland Nationals, long Metroriders and DA1, the first of the AF Optare Deltas. It has dual-purpose seating and carries the registration WLT 400.

## rpington

he next large centre is Orpington, gained from Bromley Common via Metrobus routes 1/358 or the 208, the latter somewhat roundabout. However, it is more fun to travel on an 1 which goes via Green Street Green. There are some nice spots in Farnborough on the ay, and in Green Street Green itself the Metrobus garage is passed. From here, Orpington a short journey away along Sevenoaks Road.

Centre of town is the High Street and the war memorial, and bus activity is brisk, with entish Bus, Metrobus and London Buses all well represented, the latter mostly in the form the various local Selkent Roundabout routes, operating Darts, Ivecos and several classes Mercedes from a base north of the town in Cray Avenue. Before heading north, it should e added that beyond Bromley and Orpington there are several very rural routes to investiate, either by car or with the aid of a friendly bus driver. The furthest-flung red route is the 53 West Croydon-Sevenoaks, running on summer Sundays and public holidays, and using n Olympian from Croydon garage.

## dcup Interest

rom Orpington, Sidcup provides quite a bit of interest these days. Boro'line works the 228, 33 and 492, Kentish Bus the 51/51A and 269, with independent Transcity Link on a nonndered route, the 492A.

## ctivity at Bexleyheath

erhaps the most important centre for buses in the area is Bexleyheath, subject of a major vision of services early in 1991 which has swept away the blue and white Bexleybus livy. The action is centred around the Broadway and Market Place, where an imposing ocktower keeps an eye on proceedings. The buses are many and varied. Boro'line uble-deckers appear on the 132 and 422, the former from Geddes Place where there is so a small area for bus layover. Kentish Bus is active on the busy 96 (using mainly former orthumbria Olympians), the 269 and midibus-operated local route B11. Transcity Link is w involved in the tendering process having gained the B15, on which Talbot Pullman xpress six-wheelers appear, as they do also on the company's 492A. Since the retenderg, London Central has been the dominant London bus unit, indeed it has also taken over e former Selkent Bexleyheath garage, and is using mainly Leyland Titans and Metroriders.

## WHERE TO GO, WHAT TO SEE

Below:
*Two very different midibuses bearing Roundabout fleetnames pass through the not unattractive Green Street Green in October 1990. The Carlyle-bodied Dennis Dart, DT29, is being followed by RH5, a Robin Hood-bodied Iveco Daily 49-10, on routes R1 and R5 respectively.*   Kevin Lane

Bottom:
*Boro'line Maidstone activity at Sidcup station: Leyland National 901, formerly London Buses LS 162, is on a 492, while in the background is Volvo Citybus 764 on a Swanley-bound 233 its regular haunt.*   Kevin Lane

Right:
*The main bus stops in Bexleyheath centre are situated beneath this clock tower. Slowing for pedestrians is a Transcity Link Talbot Pullman on the company's 492A to Swanley.*
Kevin Lane

## Buses to Woolwich

With the Underground non-existent in this part of London, and a British Rail service of generally only a 30min frequency on most lines, bus travel must be relied upon to get quickly
between centres. One suggestion from Bexleyheath is to take either a Kentish Bus 96 or
Boro'line 422 to Woolwich. Both travel via Plumstead, enabling a look at the Selkent garage,
a modern structure opened in 1981, replacing the former Plumstead garage and that in
Abbey Wood.

In Woolwich, head for Wellington Street and Green's End, where most services can be
seen. Kentish Bus and Boro'line are well in evidence, while London Buses operator Selkent
provides Olympians, Titans and new Optare Metroriders. Woolwich High Street is also
worth seeking out, as is the ferry across the Thames to North Woolwich where East London
reigns supreme.

## Other centres

There are other places nearby worth investigating, including Eltham, where the station forecourt is the terminus for several routes, Metrobus 61 and Boro'line 132/228/233/328 among
them. Greenwich, Charlton and Blackheath all have attractive areas for photographs,
although vehicular variety is lacking. At Greenwich there is a foot-tunnel underneath the
Thames, giving access to the Isle of Dogs at Island Gardens, southern terminus of the
Docklands Light Railway. With a little forward planning, therefore, you can make the most of
a day in London.

# South London

If I had to single out just one place to the south of London for the bus enthusiast, the
think it would be Croydon. It can be taken in two parts, east and west, each with its o
merits.

### East Croydon

By far the better train service from London is enjoyed by East Croydon, typically 16min fro
Victoria, and the station is passed by some of the services encountered at West Croydon.
George Street, immediately outside the station, pass a number of London Buses rout
including Metrorider routes 366/367, and Metrobus's tendered routes 353/354, which terr
nate round the corner outside Croydon College. Services from the south gather at the top
Park Lane and George Street and include Epsom Buses 598, East Surrey 301 and vario
London & Country routes. These will run up Wellesley Road towards West Croydon, whe
a suitable vantage point is the multi-storey car park on the corner of Poplar Walk. As t
sun could be a problem for northbound workings, an upper level is best for photography
avoid various signs and other obstructions at ground level.

### West Croydon

At West Croydon there is an open-air bus station and vehicle layover area, and an inform
tion booth also. It is quite photogenic as bus stations go, but not as good as the one tha
replaced, and that used to have London Country Routemasters as well! London Buses a
London & Country vehicles predominate, but Kentish Bus 23 to Sevenoaks also calls, as
several Green Line services. (Epsom Buses 598 leaves from Wellesley Road opposite.) Lo
don Road, outside West Croydon, is busy too: look out for a London & Country Leyla
Lynx on the tendered 289. About a mile or so along London Road is Thornton He
garage, just off the main road in Whitehall Road.

Left:
West Croydon bus station in January 1991, where a Kentish Bus B series Leyland National is substituting for a coach on Green Line service 726 to Dartford   Kevin Lane

Top:
The multi-storey car park in Wellesley Road, West Croydon, provides a suitable perch for bus watching. In this view an Epsom Buses Plaxton-bodied Bedford YMT runs in on a 598 journey from Epsom in January 1991   Kevin Lane

Above:
A busy scene in East Croydon with a London & Country Dennis Falcon working in from Reigate and Dorking, pursued by an Epsom Bus Bedford YMT, while a pair of South London Leyland Olympians complete the picture.
Kevin Lane

Above:
*Cheam Road, Sutton with the offending cinema being passed by London General Metrobus M1388 heading for Belmont in January 1991.*   Kevin Lane

Below:
*South London Metrobus M1105 turns into Mitcham Lane from Streatham High Road working a 49 from Crystal Place to Clapham Junction.*   Kevin Lane

## South of Croydon

Heading south from Croydon, the busiest route is the Brighton Road, with London Buses and London & Country well represented. South Croydon garage is about a mile down the road on the left-hand side, the present building being a 1950s reconstruction of the 1914 premises built by the LGOC but severely damaged during the war.

On to Purley, with its attractive town centre and some interesting buses, including East Surrey and Epsom Bus amid the red and green predominates. National Express also comes this way, en route from Brighton, travelling north via Thornton Heath and Streatham.

## Sutton from Purley

To the east is Sutton, reached from Purley via the 127 and 154 or 213, very much the DMS stronghold, although Metrobuses and Olympians can be found in small numbers. London & Country is also strong here and Epsom Buses appears on the 508 on Sundays. The High Street outside the station is a good spot for pictures, but the town centre is largely pedestrian only, buses running up and down the outside along St Nicholas Way and Throwley Way. There is *almost* a gem of a place for bus pictures in Cheam Road. I say almost because although there is an attractive row of half-timbered shops and the superbly restored Trinity Church, they are separated by a brick box calling itself a cinema. Whoever authorised that deserves the sack, or worse!

There are several options for Sutton: to go west will invariably mean the same DMS/London & Country diet as before, although Epsom Buses does appear hourly at Worcester Park on its service 3 from home. Epsom itself is worth a go, albeit out of the Travelcard range, or Kingston, described in the southwest section, could beckon.

Above:
*A little further south from the previous picture is the futuristic-looking Streatham garage, here with DMS2307 of Brixton garage outside.* Kevin Lane

Above:
*Plenty of Routemasters at Peckham garage in this August 1990 view! London General RML2711 stands beside Selkent RM1172 of Catford garage. Peckham garage itself opened for business in 1951.* Kevin Lane

**London Buses Variety**

However, moving north brings us to more fruitful areas such as Norwood, Streatham, Brixton, Peckham, Camberwell and Elephant & Castle. There are some leafy locations around Streatham, by St Leonard's Church for instance, while just around the corner in Streatham High Road is Streatham garage, a futuristic looking place opened in 1987 and little resembling a bus garage. Although all services in the area are in the hands of London Buses at the moment, there is a great variety. In around 20min in January 1991, the following types could be seen: DMS Metrobus (including one of the Mk 2 evaluatory vehicles), Metroride, Routemaster, Olympian, an H class Dennis Dominator (another of the evaluatory vehicles but since transferred to London Coaches), Volvo Citybus and Leyland National, in the latter two cases turning off along Mitcham Lane on routes 133 and 115 and not passing the garage. Much the same will be seen all the way up to Brixton (whose garage is in Streatham Hill, another modern-1950s-structure), with a few more, including Routemasters on the 2 and minibuses on the P4.

If you want Routemasters in some numbers outside central London, then try the 36 group from New Cross towards Peckham, Camberwell and Vauxhall (both Peckham and Camberwell have garages fronting the main road). A further temptation at Camberwell Green is the terminating 42, a tendered route operated by Kentish Bus, and more Routemasters on the 12. A little further to the south, Forest Hill and Penge are the termini of London & Country routes 78 and 176 respectively.

**Pub fare**

Bordering on to the central area, Elephant & Castle (named after a local inn) is a busy centre, with Routemasters on the 12, Volvo Citybuses on the 133, and London & Country on the 176 and numerous other routes. It is on the Underground, too, as indeed is Brixton, and is therefore easily accessible from inside London.

# South West London

For those wishing to utilise the Underground from central London, there are several choices. Richmond is as good a place as any in which to start, easily reached by the District Line (about 30min from Victoria), but also from Waterloo and the North London Line on British Rail. Kew Gardens, the stop before Richmond on the District and North London Lines, is the not unattractive terminus of the 90 from Northolt and is passed by the RH1, one of two local routes operated for the Richmond Health Authority. Both of these plus the 90 are operated by London Buslines, using Leyland Olympians and ex-Bee-Line Ford Transits respectively.

Richmond itself is interesting enough, still seeing RML operation on the 7. This and the 27/65, the latter operated by Armchair, arrive from the north over Kew Bridge and pass the Royal Botanic Gardens in Kew Road. The bus station, such as it is, can be found in Wakefield Road, reached from the station via The Quadrant, George Street and Red Lion Street. Most services call there, and the vehicle on the RH1 appears to layover here, but for more interesting pictures it is better to head for Hill Street and Bridge Street.

## Along the Thames

A quite pleasant journey is that down to Kingston, direct by Armchair 65 or via Ham on the 371 (Westlink Wright-bodied 9m Dennis Darts), with some attractive corners for photography en route.

Kingston has been a popular destination for the bus enthusiast for many years, not least because of the Smokebox bookshop in Cromwell Road. The town can boast two bus sta-

Above:
*Typical! You wait ages for a bus and then three come along at once. This is not really quite the situation here, where a number of London United Dennis Darts are seen crossing Richmond Bridge at the launch of route R70 in April 1990.* Stewart Brown

tions. By far the older is the 1928-built structure in Clarence Street, with its adjoining garage dating from 1922. Access to the bus station is through the garage, which actually closed in 1984 but which re-opened three years later in order to house minibuses for Westlink's Kingston Hoppa network. The bus station is still predominantly Westlink, although other services include London & Country 218 to Staines and 461 to Chertsey, Armchair 65 and London United's Dart-worked 285. The exit is west-facing, so is more favourable for the sun in the afternoons.

The other bus station, opened a couple of years ago, is open-air, but dull, although the long queues of passengers waiting to board the buses always makes an interesting picture. It is very busy with London Buses and London & Country services and others including Armchair's hourly 501 to Whiteley. A short way across is Eden Street, terminus of Epsom Buses' X5, Saturdays-only from Epsom District Hospital. Moving across to the other side of Kingston, try the bridge over the Thames and on to Hampton Court, the road passing between Hampton Court Park and Bushey Park, an attractive area, and busy too — routes 111/131/216, plus London & Country. The 131 is currently Westlink's only double-deck route: it uses Leyland Titans, a type hitherto not seen in this area.

Hampton Court is on the Travelcard boundary, but as the Westlink operating area is largely in Surrey, a few words on these operations will not be out of place.

## Surrey Countryside

A glance at the London bus map will reveal a number of red tentacles extending beyond the Travelcard area out into the country to such places as Bagshot, Downside and West Byfleet. Some of these services tend to be infrequent and are best pursued by car or with the aid of a sympathetic driver if you want pictures in out-of-the-way places. For an out-of-town bus centre, Staines is worth a visit. There is a modern bus station, open air, off South Street, with quite an interesting collection of operators: Westlink, London & Country, London United, Tellings-Golden Miller, London Country North West, Alder Valley, Green Line and Armchair (evenings only). Two independents work local stage services, Ashford Luxury Coaches on the 305 to Poyle (which is a little way west of Heathrow airport), generally using a former Gatwick (National Car Parks) Leyland National 2; and Tellings-Golden Miller 606 to Stanwell Moor, the regular vehicle being a Caetano-bodied Volvo B10M bus. Tellings-Golden Miller are now also active on tendered routes 116/117, using elderly Leyland Nationals numbered in the series used by the company's parent, Midland Fox, with TGM Buses fleetnames. The 305 crosses the route of London Buslines 81 to Slough near Colnbrook, a village with some pretty corners. Before leaving Staines, mention should be made of the former London & Country garage in London Road, used by Speedlink Airport Services for Jetlink and Speedlink coach services.

## Routes to Wimbledon

Wimbledon is another important centre and can be reached by British Rail from, among other places, Waterloo (12min), or by the District Line from Edgware Road. Crossing the

Above left:
*The Westlink operating area stretches deep into Surrey, and although it is well out of the Travelcard area, it is worth including in a visit. Leyland National LS335 passes the Half Moon public house, Windlesham, on a Bagshot-Staines 500 journey. There are two return trips, Monday to Friday only, on this route, only one of which actually passes the Half Moon.*
Kevin Lane

Left:
*North of Staines, several services pass through the village of Colnbrook, including London Buslines on its LT-contracted route 81 from Hounslow to Slough. Leyland Lynx D751 DLO stands beside a former London Transport bus stop in a leafy corner, belying the fact that Heathrow Airport is only a few miles to the east.* Kevin Lane

Above:
*Tooting Broadway is a busy centre, with a variety of types to be seen, including South London MCW Metrorider on routes G1 and G2. MR37 is seen in Mitcham Road in January 1991 on a Battersea-bound G1.* Kevin Lane

Thames at Putney Bridge (see the section on west London), the Putney Pier terminus of London Buslines C4 is off Lower Richmond Road. Putney garage itself (RMLs and Metrobuses) is off Putney High Street in Chelverton Road, on a site going back to horse bus days, although the present one dates from 1912, albeit much reconstructed. Route passing through Putney include London & Country 85 and the RML-worked 14, which ter minates at Putney Heath. Continuing through Roehampton and skirting Wimbledon Com mon and Richmond Park (another pleasant area for photography) we reach Kingston again or by cutting down past Tibbets Corner and through Wimbledon Village, we reach Wimble don itself. Although busy, vehicular interest is limited — the Metrobus and DMS predomi nate, although some relief is provided by the Westlink Titans on the 131 and Metroriders of London General's local Wimbledon/Mitcham route 352. Although the area around Hill Road and the Broadway looks promising for photography, traffic congestion makes life very frustrating, and I've never been too successful here.

Surbiton, a little further on from Wimbledon, is the limit of Travelcard availability on British Rail on the main line for Waterloo. Services are mainly Kingston area K routes, with Metro riders predominating, and London & Country, with an attractive location for pictures being Claremont Road with its clock tower.

## Northern Line Stops
The other Underground route into southwest London is the Northern Line to Morden, quite a trek from central London but with plenty of interesting stopping-off places on the way Elephant & Castle is a busy centre and includes Routemasters on the 12 and London Gen eral Volvo Citybuses on the 133. At Stockwell garage, with its unique arched rib concrete roof, the allocation includes RML, DMS and the Volvo Citybuses. It is situated just round the corner from Stockwell station in Binfield Road. Metroriders are encountered at Tooting

*Above:*

*The imposing façade of Morden Underground station, with a less than usual visitor in the shape of Plumstead's Olympian L136, in a red, cream and grey livery, offering a service to and from Morden railway depot. Most people seemed to prefer to travel by restored 1938 stock, myself included!* Kevin Lane

roadway on routes G1/G2, operated by South London in conjunction with Wandsworth Health Authority. Merton garage, with a largely DMS allocation, is near to Colliers Wood station in Merton High Street. A nearby outstation of Merton is Colliers Wood itself, a parking area for vehicles on the 152/200 routes.

Moving towards London, Clapham can be recommended, both Junction and Common, the latter on the Northern Line. It is all London Buses at the moment, but with some variety. Nearby, a few minutes from Wandsworth Town, London Coaches has its base in Jews Row, some of the coaching and sightseeing fleets. Up the line at Vauxhall, just to the left of the bridge, is a coach park, usually with something of interest to see.

Morden is another well-photographed place, the impressive frontage to the station providing a suitable backdrop to the passing bus scene. The DMS is very common, but London Country works the 293 Merton-Epsom as well as the 420/422, while Epsom Buses appears on the 293 on a return early morning and evening journey. Epsom, although just out of the Travelcard area, is well worth a visit, with services mostly in the hands of London Country and Epsom Buses.

## Transport at Shepperton

Where else? Shepperton, home of a certain publishing company, has some pretty parts and is served by Westlink and London & Country, while up the road in Sunbury Village, the 237 terminates from Shepherds Bush in Green Street, the Three Fishes public house being an attractive feature here. Also passing are Westlink 216/567 and Armchair 555. Plenty of scope here for good photographs. The Tolworth and Chessington area is promising, with various K routes, not to mention Epsom Buses on Epsom circular service 8 and Westlink's 468 to Ewell.

# West London

A suitable jumping off point is Hammersmith, easily accessible by the Underground (Ha
mersmith & City, District and Piccadilly Lines). Just around the corner is the south-faci
Butterwick bus station, good for photography if the sun shines, and with a small parki
area nearby. There is some variety among the London Buses representatives: Routemaste
on the 9 and 11, Leyland Lynxes on the 190, Dennis Darts on the 283 and infrequent R
with Metrobuses on what's left. Furthermore, limited-stop services, such as London
Country/Green Line to Guildford and Windsor, and Reading Transport's London servic
also call.

### Shepherds Bush

Just up the road is Shepherds Bush Green, a busy meeting point for services headi
towards central London from the west and southwest. There is plenty of activity around t
triangle surrounding the common, including Routemasters on the 11/12/88/94, the last
relatively new route started only in September 1990. Other services to look out for are t
aforementioned Dart-worked 283, and the 237 which employs G-registered Leyla
Olympians (both of these services run under the Riverside Bus name). Metrobuses are ag
well in evidence, but a welcome relief to this sea of red is provided by the orange and wh
of Armchair's Olympians on the 260, which enter along Goldhawk Road. In Wells Road, ju
before the railway bridge, is London United's Shepherds Bush garage, with its allocation
Routemasters and Metrobuses. A good viewpoint from which to look down on the fronta
of the garage can be obtained from the southbound platform of Goldhawk Road station.

South from Hammersmith is the bridge of the same name, dating from 1887, over whi
passes the 9/33/72/R6. To the southeast, and back-tracking slightly towards central Lo
don, are Fulham and Earls Court, with some pleasant architecture against which to phot
graph buses, for example along Fulham Road (Routemasters on the 14 and Lond
Buslines Mercedes on the C4) and Warwick Road (Mercedes on the 31, Metrobuses on t
74 and Optare minibuses on the C3). The Earls Court Exhibition Centre attracts plenty
coaches when open, while a favourite place to see coaches heading to and from the west
the railway bridge over the West London Line at West Kensington (also an excellent a
well known position from which to see London Underground's Lillie Bridge depot). T
bridge leads on to the Talgarth Road and Westway. The road is not used by local servi
buses, although the A1 Airbus service to Heathrow does come this way.

Left:
Hammersmith Butterwick is a stopping off point for several limited-stop services to and from the west. Bee Line Volvo/Jonckheere 789 approaches, working to Reading from Victoria.
Kevin Lane

Top:
Jostling with the traffic around Shepherds Bush Green is former Green Line coach RMC1499, now a training bus with London United, allocated round the corner at Shepherds Bush garage. Kevin Lane

Above:
West Cromwell Road, Earls Court is a good place to see coach services to the southwest; this Wilts & Dorset Leyland Tiger is caught in traffic working into Victoria from Bere Regis.
Kevin Lane

## Putney Bridge

Another nearby favourite is Putney Bridge and the District Line station, the latter the terminus of several routes including the 85, now worked by London & Country using Volvo Citybuses, and London General midibuses on the 39 operating under the Streetline name. Routes crossing Putney Bridge include the 39 and 85, as well as the 14/22 (both still Routemaster worked) and London Buslines on its C4. Buses heading south can be well photographed with All Saints' church prominent in the background. Putney itself has been dealt with in the southwest section.

## Ealing Minibuses

We haven't had much to do with minibuses yet, but a trip to Ealing will soon put that right. Ealing Broadway is well served by the Central and District Lines and is only 8min out of Paddington by British Rail. Road traffic always seems rather congested, so a trip by bus might be avoided! That said, traffic jams do have their compensations with nearly-stopped vehicles easy prey for the photographer, particularly useful in low light. Various local E routes gather outside Ealing Broadway station, and there will probably be an RW class, Wright-bodied Renault 50, complete with a Northern Ireland registration. Over the road is the terminus of the 65 to Kingston, a busy route with a 10min off-peak frequency, operated by Armchair. Opposite the station is the Haven Green terminus of the 297 to Willesden, operated since 1 December 1990 by Centrewest using Wright-bodied Dennis Darts, again carrying Northern Ireland registrations. White Leyland Lynxes of Pan Atlas will also be encountered, working the 112 to Wood Green. On passing the station heading southwards, buses turn left into The Mall. The Broadway, to the right, is again very congested and is not very distinguished, although Ealing parish church on the corner of Spring Bridge Road may make a worthwhile backdrop for pictures.

## Down Uxbridge Road

Continuing westwards along Uxbridge Road (perhaps by limited-stop 607, quicker than the usual 207), Hanwell garage is on the left, just before the clocktower off Hanwell Broadway. Its history goes back to the beginning of electric trams in London in 1901, and subsequently trolleybuses between 1935 and 1960. A little further on is Ealing Hospital which is the terminus of London Buslines route 92 from Neasden, an LT contract that started on 10 November 1990 using new Leyland Olympians. This route soon turns off the Uxbridge Road and heads north towards Greenford (the town centre of which is a fair way south of the station, so be warned!) and is quite busy with E routes, as well as Metrobuses on the 105/274, and RWs on the 282 and the aforementioned 92.

Another major centre is Uxbridge, served by the Metropolitan Line, with a train every 15min, off-peak. The railway station is well worth a second glance, with its imposing architecture featuring stained-glass windows, while the bus station, based around a turning circle, lies adjacent in Bakers Road. Centrewest's garage too is here, a modern building opened in November 1983, replacing increasingly inadequate facilities out of town in Denham. There is plenty of activity at Uxbridge but little variety. Local U-Line routes are dominated by the MA class, Alexander-bodied Mercedes 811Ds, while the 207/222/223/607 are in the hands of Metrobuses. Several London Country North West routes also converge

Above left:
*Southbound buses crossing Putney Bridge keep to a bus lane, making photography without other traffic getting in the way quite easy. Putney-allocated RML2383 is seen on a 14 in December 1990.* Kevin Lane

Left:
*A pair of Centrewest RW class Wright-bodied Renault 50s on local E routes are pictured outside Ealing Broadway station in December 1990. A London & Country Leyland Atlantean can be seen in the background on a 65, now in the hands of Armchair.* Kevin Lane

in the town. Leyland Nationals seem popular, although the recent take-over by Luton & District may well bring changes. Limited-stop services calling at Uxbridge include Green Line and City of Oxford. If the bus station is less than inspiring, the High Street is better because a multi-storey car park gives a variety of views from its different levels. Most services loop round to behind the Pavilions Shopping Centre in Oxford Road, the windswept walkways affording more slightly aerial views of the buses below. Unfortunately, the old town, glimpsed behind the concrete is avoided by buses. There are some more rural corners but the main road through Cowley and Yiewsley is generally dull. West Drayton is better, but again vehicular interest is limited, to Metrobuses on the 222/223 and MAs on the U3/U5.

### Stop Before Heathrow

The easiest way to get from central London to Heathrow Airport is by the Piccadilly Line (journey time around 50min with a train every 5-10min). Hounslow is well worth a stop over on the way. Alighting at Hounslow East and turning left into Kingsley Road, the bus station and garage is a few minutes' walk. Departing services face west before turning south into the High Street and there is much to see: London Buslines works the 81 to Slough (usually a Lynx but sometimes a DMS), as well as midibus route 201, while a newcomer is Tellings-Golden Miller on the 116/117. London Buses provides the remaining interest. Westlink works several services, notably the 110, the preserve of the Optare Delta. The Dennis Dart has been increasingly more evident in the area, with several Harrier routes now in operation — H21/H22/H23/H98, all of which call at the bus station. Other services tend to be Metrobus-worked, although the 237, Riverside Bus, is Olympian (but this passes along London Road and the High Street and does not call at the bus station). Continuing along the High Street, the junction with Lampton Road and Bell Road brings contact with the H20, not part of the Harrier network, but a local service between Hounslow Civic Centre and Ivybridge, operated by Westlink using CVE Omni minibuses actually owned by the London Borough of Hounslow. The Piccadilly Line can be regained here at Hounslow Central, or continuing along Bath Road will bring you to Hounslow West, which has an attractive frontage for services, including the 81 and H98.

Below:
*Hatton Cross, the last stop on the Piccadilly Line before Heathrow, is always worth a look. London United Dennis Dart DT150 on an H23 together with a former Alder Valley South Leopard working for Armchair on its 556 to Walton-on-Thames provide the interest in November 1990.* Kevin Lane

Below:
*And so to Heathrow. A couple of Airbus Metrobuses stand at Terminal 4, viewed from the nearby car park.* Kevin Lane

# WHERE TO GO, WHAT TO SEE

Before reaching Heathrow, it is worthwhile spending a short time at Hatton Cross, situated on the eastern edge of the airport. A small bus station adjoins the Underground station, and this sees a variety of services including London Buslines, this time on the 90 (Kew Gardens station-Northolt station) using G-registered Leyland Olympians, Armchair on its 555/556/557, Green Line 726/727, as well as London United Metroriders on the 202/203 and Darts on the 285. An excellent vantage point is a footbridge over Eastchurch Road which gives a good overall view of the bus station, vehicles arriving towards you before swinging away to the stops. Furthermore, coaches to or from Terminal 4 pass nearby and can be photographed from the bridge also.

### Heathrow Terminal 4
The next stop on the Underground is Heathrow Terminal 4, set apart from the main airport complex. A foretaste of what can be sampled at the central area terminals include Airbus services A1/A2, the Rail-Air links to Reading (in the hands of Alder Valley) and to Woking (operated by Frames Rickards), and also the Speedlink service to Gatwick Airport, the Jetlink 747 from Luton Airport to Gatwick (operated by Speedlink), and Flights' Flightlink service from Manchester and Birmingham. The various inter-terminal and free car park services (to be described below) also call. Operations are carried out on two levels, the ground for arrivals, first floor for departures. Photography is made easy by adjacent multi-storey car parks, allowing views down on to some bus stops, although others are under cover and require quite lengthy exposures.

Now to Terminals 1, 2 and 3, next and last stop on the Underground. Bus-wise it can be quite fascinating, if a little bewildering to the inexperienced. Hopefully I can shed some light!

### Heathrow Central
Arriving by Underground or by service bus or coach, one will find the bus station a pretty straightforward affair, with separate parts for National Express, other coach and local bus services, only the first of which is totally under cover. There is also limited space for vehicle layover.

*A rarity at Heathrow are Scania K112s with Van Hool dual-door, dual-purpose bodies operating to the long-term car parks, also a free service. They are owned by Capital Coaches and work for British Airways. Kevin Lane*

Above:
*Heathrow attracts a large number of National Express and other coach services. Waiting at the bus station in December 1990 is an MAN of Pike, Andover working a 515 journey between Poole and Victoria.*   Kevin Lane

National Express services are many and various, with arrivals from all over the country, giving a wide variety of operators to look out for. Those passing to/from South Wales and the West Country predominate. It can get very busy, particularly in the summer, and as such can be a fascinating place for observation. A number of limited-stop services also converge on Heathrow, those listed above for Terminal 4 (some of which call at the bus station), and also United Counties' Coachlinks X1 and Green Line 726 to name others.

Local services include London & Country 436 from Guildford (numbered 536 and worked by Alder Valley on Sundays), Armchair 555 from Chertsey, and 556/557 from Walton/Weybridge; and London Buses routes 105/140/223/285/U5 and night route N97 to distant Liverpool Street station. The bus station is also a picking up point for staff buses conveying aircrew to and from the various terminals.

## Internal Services

A prominent part of the airport scene are the many internal bus services; inter-terminal, between car parks, staff transfer, etc. British Airways would appear to be the main operator of such vehicles, with a number of Wadham-Stringer-bodied Dodge G10s, and, of a more exotic nature, Scania K112CRBs with yellow East Lancs dual-purpose bodies complete with large air-operated luggage doors. These latter vehicles see use between Terminals 1 and 4. Some work is contracted out to Capital Coaches, whose work also includes inter-terminal work as well as to and from long-term car parks. Familiar types to be encountered are Leyland National 2s, Scania K112DRBs with Van Hool DP30D bodies, and Plaxton bus-bodied Volvo B10Ms. These and other types can be seen aplenty within a short distance of the bus station, although it is more rewarding to explore the various areas using the walkways that connect terminals with car parks. With a medium or long telephoto lens some exciting pictures can be taken. Perhaps the ultimate is to get both bus and plane in the one shot — not so easy! I have only dealt with the landside buses as those working airside are of course out of bounds, although such delights as an Optare Delta or a MAN Articulated may be glimpsed from the viewing area on the Queen's Building.

117

## North West London

The northwest of London is quite well served by the Underground, which can be used to some advantage. We can begin at West Hampstead, which has three railway stations with a few hundred yards along West End Lane: Thameslink, North London Line and the Underground in the shape of the Jubilee Line. West End Lane is busy enough, with Routemaster on the 159, Mercedes-Benz/Alexander midibuses on the 28, and the C11, now in the hands of R&I Tours, using Dennis Darts. The  northern terminus of the 159 is a little way along West End Lane, under the trees near to the fire station. At Willesden Green, the next station but one on, we encounter Metrobus-worked 266 (from Cricklewood garage, so that one of the first batch, M1-M5, may turn up) and an Armchair Olympian on the 260. The station frontage is rather attractive, recalling its Metropolitan Railway origins, and is a good backdrop for pictures. Turning right out of the station and into the High Road will lead to Willesden garage, itself the terminus of a couple of interesting routes, the RML-worked 6, and the 297, which was the first London route to receive Wright-bodied Dennis Darts. Carlyle-bodied Darts appear on the 206. The 297 is also found further along the line at both Neasden and Wembley Park stations. There are several options from Wembley Park — a trip up the Stanmore branch for Pan Atlas 107, which terminates at Queensbury station where London Buslines 79 and BTS 114 pass. Canons Park for London Buslines and the 79 again, and London Country North West for the 340; and Stanmore itself for the Dart-worked 251.

Above:
*Metroline RML2668 is pictured in Willesden High Road, a short way from its home garage, Willesden, where it will terminate on a 6 from Hackney Wick.*   Kevin Lane

**Above:**
*Queensbury station on the Jubilee Line sees Northern Counties-bodied Leyland Olympians on LT-tendered services from three operators. Pan Atlas route 107 terminates from New Barnet, while the two seen here are London Buslines on the 79 and BTS on the 114.*
*Kevin Lane*

## Edgware

It is only a short walk from Canons Park to Edgware (an obvious photogenic feature en route is the parish church of Little Stanmore, there's a bus stop outside), with its bus/rail interchange and garage. The Northern Line terminus is rather more distinguished, architecturally, than the bus station next door, but the latter is busy with Darts on the 251/288, London Country North West on the 142/340, Pan Atlas on the 107 and London Buslines appearing on the 79. BTS double-deckers work the 292 and London Buses Metrobuses are on everything else. This is a good place for photographs! There is also a bus station attached to Mill Hill Broadway Thameslink station a mile or two away, but it is all under cover and is a bit of a dead loss, despite some variety in the shape of the Darts on the 251 and the BTS-worked 114. A better bet for these two services is Burnt Oak Broadway, the next station down from Edgware.

## Buses to Brent Cross

Further south is the 'North West End', Brent Cross Shopping Centre, naturally a focal point for services, although not outside shopping hours. Buses circulate outside the entrance, including Pan Atlas on the 112, London Country North West on the 142, Grey Green with its single-deck Volvo B10Ms (impressive machines) on the 210, and R&I Tours on the C11. Nearby is Staples Corner, the end of the M1 motorway, traffic bound for central London taking the North Circular Road and Hendon Way, with some coach services calling at stops just to the east of the shopping centre.

## Variety at Golders Green

Even more interesting is Golders Green, for a long time a favourite place to observe buses. The bus station is next to the Underground station and is always interesting. Routemasters are now only to be seen on the 13, while independents on LT tendered routes are R&I Tours with Ivecos on the 168 and H2, Grey Green on the 210 and Armchair working the 260.

**Above:**
*Independent activity at Golders Green: a Brent Cross-bound 210, in the charge of a Grey Green Volvo, passes an Armchair Olympian on a 260. R&I Tours is also active on the H2 and 268.*   Kevin Lane

everything else is virtually all Metrobus, although Gold Arrow route 28 with its DW and MA Mass midibuses terminates here from Wandsworth. In addition to all this, Golders Green is an important National Express stop for services to and from the north. The bus station is acceptable for photography, but it is better to position yourself either at the entrance at the junction of Finchley, Golders Green and North End Roads, or the exit in North End Road. The nearby clock-tower provides a useful photographic feature, in particular for buses arriving along Finchley Road.

Another attractive terminus is Hampstead Heath, South End Green, with Belsize Park the nearest tube. Turn right on leaving the station and then right again into Pond Street and down the short hill. An immediate photographic plus is the monument seen as you approach. As for the buses, South End Green is host to Grey Green 24/168 and R&I Tours C11/C12 as well as the 46 of London Northern. Hampstead as a whole has many good places for photography, The Spaniards Inn for the 210 (Grey Green) and Jack Straw's Castle for the 210 and R&I 268 to name but two.

## Harrow

Back at Wembley Park, it is a short journey on the Metropolitan Line to Harrow-on-the-Hill, with its modern bus station next door. Services are mixed with extra colour from Sovereign on the H11/H17, BTS on the 114 and London Country North West working the 258/340, as

**Left:**
*It is worth looking out for details of railway engineering work, which often involves a temporary replacement bus service. London Underground tends, understandably, to use London Buses, but British Rail is more likely to patronise a local independent operator. Chalfont Coaches was among those chosen when work was being carried out near Willesden Junction in March 1985, where this Ford R1114 was on hand.*   Kevin Lane

Above:
*Right on the edge of the Travelcard area, Northwood plays host to several services includi*
*London Country North West's 347/348 from Abbots Langley towards Uxbridge. Calling at*
*the station in June 1990 was Leyland Olympian LR49.*   Kevin Lane

well as the various 'Harrow Hoppa' midibus routes of Metroline. With the demise of the e
West Midlands Ailsas, London Buses double-deckers are currently all Metrobuses. T
town centre is not particularly exciting as far as photogenic locations are concerne
although College Road and Peterborough Road are adequate. Perhaps it is better to get c
of town: High Street, past Harrow School, is attractive for the H11 and 258 for instan
while even further out, Pinner Green and Northwood spring to mind, the latter the termin
of Sovereign's H11, as well as getting a visit from London Country North West's 347
Uxbridge-Abbots Langley services and Centrewest's 282, the preserve of Wright-bodi
Renault 50s. We are getting close to Watford, with W routes at South Oxhey nearby
although out of the scope of this book. (The LT tendered 258 does reach Watford Juncti
from South Harrow.)

## Rural Ruislip

Back to Harrow-on-the-Hill, the Uxbridge branch can be taken to Ruislip, where there
more variety than in many larger towns. The bus stops are situated outside the stati
(which is a listed building) and currently include Scorpio on its 398 (which could produce
Leyland National), BTS on the 114 (which extends to Ruislip Lido on Sundays) and
Sovereign Mercedes on the H11; plus the U1, E2 (Sundays), and E7. Do not confine yours
just to the station, but head up through the town towards Ruislip Common and the Lid
Indeed, we are very much in 'Metroland' and as such there are many rural corners for b
photography — just look at the number of green areas on the map in Bus Guide 15. It
logical to continue on the Metropolitan to Uxbridge, although this is covered in the secti
dealing with west London.

Right:
*Sovereign Bus & Coach is a new operator to the Harrow area, its route H10 starting on*
*19 January 1991. Two weeks later, Mercedes H419 FGS is seen at Rayners Lane.*
Kevin Lane

# APPENDICES

# London Buses vehicle types

**Double-decks**

| Code | Type |
|------|------|
| DMS | Daimler Fleetline |
| L | Leyland Olympian |
| M | Metrobus |
| RM | Routemaster |
| RMA | Forward-entrance Routemaster |
| RMC | Routemaster coach |
| RML | Long Routemaster |
| S | Scania N113DRB/Alexander |
| T | Leyland Titan |
| V | Volvo Ailsa |
| VC | Volvo Citybus/Northern Counties |

**Single-deck**

| Code | Type |
|------|------|
| BL | Bristol LH6L/ECW[1] |
| DA | DAF SB220/Optare Delta |
| DRL | 9.8m Dennis Dart/Reeve Burgess |
| DWL | 9m Dennis Dart/Wright |
| LS | Leyland National |
| LX | Leyland Lynx |

**Midibuses**

| Code | Type |
|------|------|
| CV | CVE Omni |
| DR | Dennis Dart/Reeve Burgess |
| DT | Dennis Dart/Carlyle |
| DW | Dennis Dart/Wright |
| FR | Iveco 49.10/Reeve Burgess |
| FS | Ford Transit |
| MA | Mercedes 811D/Alexander |
| MC | Mercedes 811D/Carlyle |
| MR | Metrorider |
| MRL | Long Metrorider[2] |
| MT | Mercedes 811D/Reeve Burgess |
| MW | Mercedes 811D/Wrights |
| OV | Optare CityPacer |
| RB | Renault S75/Reeve Burgess |
| RH | Iveco 49.10/Robin Hood |
| RW | Renault S75/Wrights |
| SR | Optare StarRider |

**London Coaches**

| Code | Type |
|------|------|
| DD | DAF/Duple coach |
| DV | DAF/Van Hool coach |
| ERM | Extended Routemaster (open-top) |
| H | Dennis Dominator/Northern Counties |
| RCL | Long Routemaster coach |
| RM | Routemaster (some open-top) |
| RMA | Forward-entrance Routemaster |
| RMC | Routemaster coach |

[1]Now used for training only
[2]Early examples built by MCW, later ones by Optare

# London Buses garages

## London Central

| Garage | Code | Types allocated | Peak vehicle output |
|---|---|---|---|
| Bexleyheath[1] | BX | MR, MRL, SR, T | 72 |
| Camberwell | Q | RM, RML, SR, T | 110 |
| New Cross | NX | L, SR, T | 90 |
| Peckham | PM | LS, RM, RML, SR, T | 126 |

## Selkent

| Garage | Code | Types allocated | Peak vehicle output |
|---|---|---|---|
| Bromley | TB | LS, MRL, T | 78 |
| Catford | TL | DW, MW, RM, SR, T | 128 |
| Orpington | OB | DT, MC, RH | 26 |
| Plumstead | PD | L, MRL, T | 118 |

## South London

| Garage | Code | Types allocated | Peak vehicle output |
|---|---|---|---|
| Brixton | BN | RM, RML, DMS | 59 |
| Croydon | TC | DMS, L | 102 |
| Norwood | N | L, RML, T | 60 |
| Streatham | AK | DR, M, MR | 80 |
| Thornton Heath | TH | DMS, DT, L | 91 |

## London General

| Garage | Code | Types allocated | Peak vehicle output |
|---|---|---|---|
| Merton | AL | DR, M | 110 |
| Putney | AF | M, MA, RML | 79 |
| Stockwell | SW | DR, M, RML, VC | 113 |
| Sutton | A | DMS, DW, M, MR | 83 |
| Victoria | GM | M, RM, RML | 73 |
| Victoria Basement[2] | GB | CV, OV, SR, MA, MRL | 55 |
| Waterloo (Red Arrow) | RA | LS | 47 |

## London United

| Garage | Code | Types allocated | Peak vehicle output |
|---|---|---|---|
| Fulwell | FW | DT, M | 110[3] |
| Hounslow | AV | DR, DT, FR, LS, M | 100 |
| Shepherds Bush | S | M, RML | 87 |
| Stamford Brook | V | DT, DW, L, LX, M | 61 |

## CentreWest

| Garage | Code | Types allocated | Peak vehicle output |
|---|---|---|---|
| Alperton | ON | DW, M | 44 |
| Hanwell | HL | M, MA, MT, RW | 112 |
| Acton | AT | RW | 20[4] |
| Uxbridge | UX | M, MA | 75 |
| Westbourne Park | X | DW, M, MA, RM, RML | 130 |

## Metroline

| Garage | Code | Types allocated | Peak vehicle output |
|---|---|---|---|
| Cricklewood | W | M | 34 |
| Edgware | EW | DT, M, SR | 74 |
| Harrow Weald | HD | DT, LS, M | 48 |
| North Wembley[5] | NW | DT | 30 |
| Willesden | AC | DT, M, RML | 63 |

## London Northern

| Garage | Code | Types allocated | Peak vehicle output |
|---|---|---|---|
| Chalk Farm | CF | T | 61 |
| Finchley | FY | M, RML, T | 66 |
| Holloway | HT | M, RM, RML | 107 |
| Potters Bar | PB | M, MR, S, SR, V | 74 |

## Leaside

| Garage | Code | Types allocated | Peak vehicle output |
|---|---|---|---|
| Enfield | E | M | 84 |
| Hackney<br>(from 23 November 1991) | CT | MRL, RML | 52 |
| Palmers Green | AD | M | 43 |
| Stamford Hill | SF | M | 60 |
| Tottenham | AR | M, RML | 86 |
| Wood Green | WN | M, DW | 90 |

## London Forest

| Garage | Code | Types allocated | Peak vehicle output |
|---|---|---|---|
| Ash Grove[6] | AG | LS, RML, T | 100 |
| Walthamstow[6] | WW | MR, MRL, T | 74 |

## East London

| Garage | Code | Types allocated | Peak vehicle output |
|---|---|---|---|
| Barking | BK | T | 72 |
| Bow | BW | RB, RML, T | 109 |
| Leyton<br>(from 23 November 1991) | T | LS, T | 47 |
| Romford | NS | LS[7], T | 50 |
| Seven Kings | AP | T | 48 |
| Upton Park | U | T, RMC, RML | 86 |
| West Ham | WH | LS, T | 89 |

## Stanwell Buses

| Garage | Code | Types allocated | Peak vehicle output |
|---|---|---|---|
| Hounslow | SB | CV, DA, FS, LS | 33[8] |
| Kingston | SB | DWL, LS, MR, MRL, T | 52 |

These figures apply generally to the situation as at 1 June 1991, though some adjustment has taken place to take into account changing circumstances since that date. Peak vehicle output does not account for spare buses so the actual number of vehicles at each garage will be slightly larger.

As at 1 June the peak output of buses was 4,144, of which 610 were Routemasters, 2,619 other double-deck types (171 DMSs, 234 Olympians, 1,250 Metrobuses, 919 Titans, nine Scanias, three Ailsas and 33 Volvo Citybuses), 130 single-deckers and 785 midibuses.

[1] Taken over from Selkent
[2] Central London Midibuses
[3] Estimated figure, including 30 Ms transferred from Norbiton on its closure on 6 September 1991.
[4] Acton is the former Acton Tram Depot reopened as a midibus base, as an outstation of Hanwell. It operates Ealing-area route E3
[5] North Wembley is an outstation of Harrow Weald, operating routes H12, H14-16 and 187
[6] London Forest closed down on 23 November 1991, and Ash Grove and Walthamstow both closed. Its two other garages, Hackney and Leyton, are shown under their new units, Leaside and East London respectively
[7] Two Mobility Buses only
[8] This figure applies to the situation prior to the retendering of routes 116/7, 203, which involved 21 vehicles. However some additional work has been taken on since the loss of those routes, but not sufficient to make up the loss.

# Tendered services

This table shows London Transport tendered services, operated by non-London Buses companies, though it includes services operated by Westlink.

| Route | Operator | Contract start date |
|---|---|---|
| 20 Walthamstow-Debden | Grey-Green | tba |
| 22<sup>A</sup> Clapton Park-London Bridge Station | Kentish Bus | 20.01.90 |
| 22<sup>B</sup> Homerton Hospital-Piccadilly Circus | Kentish Bus | 24.02.90 |
| 24 Hampstead Heath-Pimlico | Grey-Green | 06.11.88 |
| *42 Aldgate-Camberwell Green | Kentish Bus | 07.02.87 |
| 51/51<sup>A</sup> Woolwich-Orpington/Swanley | Kentish Bus | 16.08.86 |
| 55 Clapton-Tottenham Court Road Station | Kentish Bus | 24.02.90 |
| 61 Bromley-Chislehurst | Metrobus | 16.08.86 |
| 65 Ealing-Kingston | Armchair | 26.01.91 |
| 66 Leytonston-Romford | County Bus | 04.08.90 |
| 78 Shoreditch-Forest Hill | London & Country | 10.11.90 |
| 79 Edgware-Alperton | London Buslines | 21.11.87 |
| 81 Hounslow-Slough | London Buslines | 13.07.85 |
| 85 Putney Bridge Station-Kingston | London & Country | 29.09.90 |
| 90 Kew Gardens Station-Northolt | London Buslines | 19.08.89 |
| 92 Southall, Ealing Hospital-Neasden | London Buslines | 10.11.90 |
| 96 Woolwich-Dartford | Kentish Bus | 19.01.91 |
| 97 Chingford-Leyton | Ensign Citybus | autumn 91 |
| 97A Chingford-Walthamstow | Ensign Citybus | 14.09.91 |
| 103 Rainham-North Romford | Grey-Green | 06.01.91 |
| 107 Queensbury-New Barnet Station | Atlas Bus | 07.10.89 |
| 108 Wanstead-Lewisham | Boro'line, Maidstone | 25.11.89 |
| 110 Twickenham-Cranford | Westlink | 28.04.90 |
| 112 Ealing Broadway-Wood Green | Atlas Bus | 30.07.88 |
| 114 Ruislip-Harrow-Mill Hill | BTS Coaches | 19.01.91 |
| 116 Brentford-Hounslow-Bedfont | Tellings Golden Miller | 10.08.91 |
| 117 Brentford-Ashford-Staines | Tellings Golden Miller | 10.08.91 |
| 123 Wood Green-Ilford | Ensign Citybus | autumn 91 |
| 125 Finchley Central-Winchmore Hill | Grey-Green | 14.11.87 |
| 127 Selsdon-Tooting Broadway | London & Country | 22.03.86 |
| 131 West Molesey-Wimbledon | Westlink | 29.09.90 |
| 132 Bexleyheath-Eltham | Boro'line Maidstone | 16.01.88 |
| 141 Wood Green-Moorgate | Grey-Green | 02.92 |
| 142 Watford Junction-Brent Cross | Luton & District | 21.06.86 |
| 144 Turnpike Lane-Chingford | County Bus | autumn 91 |
| 146 Bromley-Downe | Metrobus | 10.08.91 |
| 158 Chingford-Stratford | Ensign Citybus | autumn 91 |
| 167 Ilford-Loughton | Grey-Green | tba |
| 168 Hampstead Heath-Waterloo | Grey-Green | 22.09.90 |
| 173 Stratford-Becontree Heath | Grey-Green | 28.02.87 |
| 176 Oxford Circus-Penge | London & Country | 10.11.90 |
| 179 Barking-Chingford | Grey-Green | 17.10.87 |
| *193 Romford-Hornchurch | Thamesway | 13.07.85 |
| 201 Staines-Hounslow | London Buslines | 10.08.91* |
| 203 Staines-Stanwell-Brentford | London Buslines | 10.08.91* |
| 210 Finsbury Park-Brent Cross | Grey-Green | 22.09.90 |
| $212 Chingford-Walthamstow | Ensign Citybus | autumn 91 |
| 215 Yardley Lane-Walthamstow | Ensign Citybus | 14.09.91 |
| 228/328 Eltham-Chislehurst-Eltham | Boro'line Maidstone | 16.01.88 |
| 233 Swanley-Eltham | Boro'line Maidstone | 16.01.88 |
| 235 Woodford Wells-Leytonstone Station (schooldays) | Thamesway | 06.03.89 |
| 246 Harold Hill-Corbets Tey | Ensign Citybus | 24.09.88 |
| 248 Cranham-Upminster-Romford | Ensign Citybus | 01.07.89 |
| 252 Collier Row-Romford-Gidea Park | Ensign Citybus | 01.07.89 |
| 256 Hornchurch, St George's Hospital-Harold Hill | County Bus | 29.09.90 |
| 258 Watford-South Harrow | Luton & District | 19.01.91 |

| Route | Operator | Date |
|---|---|---|
| 260 North Finchley-Shepherds Bush | Armchair | 23.06.90 |
| 261 Green Street Green-Lewisham | Metrobus | 21.11.87 |
| *268 Golders Green-Finchley Road Station | R & I Coaches | 03.06.89 |
| 269 Bexleyheath-Bromley North | Kentish Bus | 19.01.91 |
| 272 Woolwich-Thamesmead | Boro'line Maidstone | 24.11.90 |
| 275 Walthamstow-Barkingside | Grey-Green | tba |
| 289 Elmers End Green-Purley | London & Country | 07.02.87 |
| 292 Borehamwood-Edgware-Colindale | BTS Coaches | 22.02.88 |
| 298 South Mimms-Turnpike Lane | Grey-Green | 22.02.88 |
| *299 South Mimms-Southgate | Ensign Citybus | 02.92 |
| 307 Barnet, Arkley Hotel-Brimsdown | Thamesway | 27.09.86 |
| 313 Potters Bar-Chingford | Grey-Green | 22.02.88 |
| 320 Bromley North-Westerham | London & Country | 01.09.90 |
| $320 Bromley North-Biggin Hill (Sunday service) | Kentish Bus | 26.11.89 |
| 340 South Harrow-Harrow | Luton & District | 19.01.91 |
| *346 Upminster Station-Upminster Park Estate | County Bus | 29.09.90 |
| 353 Orpington-Croydon | Metrobus | 16.08.86 |
| 354 Bromley-Selsdon-Croydon | Metrobus | 16.08.86 |
| 357 Orpington-Forestdale-Croydon | Metrobus | 16.08.86 |
| 359 Hammond Street-Manor House | Thamesway | 21.01.87 |
| 361 Bromley-Green Street Green | Metrobus | 16.08.86 |
| *362 Chadwell Heath-Barkingside | Thamesway | 01.12.90 |
| *371 Richmond-Kingston | Westlink | 29.09.90 |
| 379 Chingford-Yardley Lane Estate | Thamesway | 05.03.89 |
| 422 Woolwich-Bexleyheath | Boro'line Maidstone | 26.11.88 |
| 446 Corbets Tey-Cranham | Ensign Citybus | 24.09.88 |
| 471 Orpington Station-Green Street Green | Kentish Bus | 21.08.89 |
| 472 Woolwich-Thamesmead (Saturdays) | Boro'line Maidstone | 24.11.90 |
| 492 Sidcup-Dartford | Boro'line Maidstone | 26.11.88 |
| 493 Orpington-Ramsden Estate | London & Country | 17.08.91 |
| 550 Gidea Park-Cranham | Ensign Citybus | 03.07.89 |
| 911-919/930 Croydon Mobility Bus routes | Kentish Bus | 19.01.91 |
| *B11 Bexleyheath-Abbey Wood | Kentish Bus | 19.01.91 |
| *B12 Bexleyheath-Erith | Kentish Bus | 19.01.91 |
| *B15 Welling Corner-Bexleyheath- | Transcity | 19.01.91 |
| *C4 Hurlingham-Putney Pier | London Buslines | 01.04.89 |
| C11 Archway-Brent Cross | R & I Coaches | 21.07.90 |
| C12 King's Cross-Finchley Road Station | R & I Coaches | 21.07.90 |
| *H2 Golders Green-Hampstead | R & I Coaches | 10.06.89 |
| *H10 Harrow (circular) | Sovereign | 19.01.91 |
| *H11 Northwick Park Hospital-Norwood Statio | Sovereign | 01.12.90 |
| *H13 Ruislip Lido-Northwood Hills | Sovereign | 01.12.90 |
| *H17 Harrow-Sudbury | Sovereign | 16.02.91 |
| *K1 New Malden-Surbiton | Westlink | 27.06.87 |
| *K2 Hook-Kingston Hospital | Westlink | 27.06.87 |
| *K3 Kingston Hospital-Lower Green | Westlink | 27.06.87 |
| *K4 Kingston-Hook | Westlink | 02.12.89 |
| *K5 Kingston-New Malden | Westlink | 07.12.89 |
| *K6 Ham-Roehampton Vale | Westlink | 02.12.89 |
| N99 Chadwell Heath-Romford-Cranham | Ensign Citybus | 27.03.87 |
| *P14 Surrey Quays Station-Cubitt Town | Kentish Bus | 19.11.88 |
| *W6 Picketts Lock-Southgate | Ensign Citybus | 02.92 |
| *W9 Enfield-Muswell Hill | Thamesway | 13.07.85 |
| *W11 Walthamstow-Billet Road | Thamesway | 23.11.91 |
| W12 Walthamstow-Wanstead | Thamesway | 23.11.91 |
| W13 Woodford Wells-Leytonstone Station | Thamesway | 04.03.89 |
| *W14 Claybury Hospital-Leytonstone Station | County | tba |
| *W15 Walthamstow-Hackney Central | County Bus | 23.11.91 |
| *W16 Chingford Mount-Leytonstone | County Bus | 23.11.91 |

KEY:
* Midibus operated
$ Tendered on Sundays only